Press Freedoms Under Pressure

Report of the Twentieth Century Fund Task Force
on the Government and the Press

Background Paper by Fred P. Graham

The Twentieth Century Fund/New York/1972

Library of Congress Catalog Card No. 72-80586
SBN 87078-125-1
Copyright © 1972 by the Twentieth Century Fund, Inc.
Manufactured in the United States of America

ii

Foreword

The Twentieth Century Fund, which is sponsoring a series of book-length studies and shorter reports on various aspects of communications as part of its research program, assembled the independent Task Force on Press Freedoms in February 1971. It immediately began its studies and deliberations. In fact, it had all but completed its report when the publication of the Pentagon Papers took place. The fundamental issues raised by that event and all that followed, led the Task Force to extend and revamp its work so that it could take into account the significance of that event to the press and the public.

The Task Force's work was enlivened by two other controversies involving the government and the press that erupted in the course of its own debate. One was the broadcasting of "The Selling of the Pentagon," which led to hearings by a Congressional subcommittee. The other was the action of the Supreme Court in granting a writ of certiorari to Earl Caldwell of the *New York Times,* who refused to enter a grand jury room to testify about the Black Panthers.

Because of these developments, the Task Force decided to release its findings and recommendations in November 1971, well in advance of final publication. Its report received a great deal of attention in the media. But the issues it deals with are of more than momentary significance. Accordingly, the Fund is publishing the final version of the Task Force report along with a factual background paper by Fred P. Graham of *The New York Times,* who also served as rapporteur for the Task Force. (Mr. Graham, however, played no part in the preparation of the section dealing with the Pentagon Papers.)

Both the Task Force and the Fund regret that the Honorable Shirley Hufstedler of the Ninth Circuit Court of Appeals had to resign from the Task Force before completion of its work to avoid a possible conflict in the event that issues covered in the report came before her court. While on the Task Force she was a most active and valuable member, demonstrating a keen awareness of the intricate problems affecting the law and the media, so that her departure was greatly regretted.

Although the Task Force did not always reach agreement, its discussions were completely candid, full and productive. The important roles played by Judge Robert Williamson, the chairman, and Mr. Graham, the rapporteur, deserve special mention; but every member of the Task Force merits a tribute for concern and dedication. The Fund is grateful to them all.

M. J. Rossant, DIRECTOR
The Twentieth Century Fund
March 1972

Contents

Members of the Task Force

Jack Bass
Bureau Chief
CHARLOTTE OBSERVER, Columbia, S.C.

Ralph de Toledano
Columnist
Washington, D.C.

Thomas King Forcade
Washington Representative
Underground Press Syndicate, Washington

Bert H. Early
Executive Director
American Bar Association, Chicago

Norman Isaacs
Editor in Residence
Columbia University, New York Ctiy

L. F. Palmer, Jr.
Columnist
CHICAGO DAILY NEWS, Chicago

George E. Reedy
Author
Smithsonian Institution, Washington

Roger Rook
District Attorney
Clackamas County Courthouse, Oregon City, Oregon

Mike Wallace
Correspondent
CBS News, New York City

Robert Williamson
Former Chief Justice of Maine
Augusta, Maine

Howard B. Woods
Editor and Publisher
ST. LOUIS SENTINEL, St. Louis

Fred P. Graham, *Rapporteur and Author of*
Background Paper
THE NEW YORK TIMES, New York City

REPORT OF THE TASK FORCE

"Where men cannot freely convey their thoughts to one another, no other liberty is secure; the way is barred for making common cause against encroachments . . . Free expression is thus unique among liberties as protector and promoter of the others . . . The meaning of a free press is inseparable from the general meaning of freedom in the modern state."
— William Ernest Hocking

"The First Amendment presupposes that right conclusions are more likely to be gathered out of a multitude of tongues than through any kind of authoritative selection. To many this is, and will always be, folly; but we have staked upon it our all."
— Learned Hand

Introduction

Farsighted though they were, James Madison, John Adams and Thomas Jefferson, who led the battle for adoption of the Bill of Rights, could not possibly have envisioned what the years ahead were to hold for the nation they were founding. Theirs was a country of just over three million people and an inhospitable wilderness. There were just 32 newspapers in all of the country; total circulation, at most, was 40,000 a week. To the nation's founders, journalism was as much Tom Paine's *Common Sense* and the "Crisis" papers as newspapers struggling to exist. The passage of the Stamp Act that placed a tax on papers and the drama of John Peter Zenger's trial that centered on freedom of the press were still fresh.

It was not possible, those 200 years ago, to foresee a nation of more than 200 million people, of 1,750 daily newspapers with 65 million copies each day rolling from their presses, of magazines of infinite variety numbering more than 200 million copies each month, and of ubiquitous radio and television. Even Jefferson, that Renaissance man of his time, would not have speculated about electronic communication, much less one that reaches al-

3

most every home with the power to bring sight and sound from American explorers on the moon.

Yet it is reasonable to believe that were they with us today, Jefferson and his colleagues would acknowledge and accept radio and television as integral arms of the press. For the founders of the Republic felt themselves to be inheritors of a great tradition. They were acutely aware that the intellectual revolution launched in the middle of the fifteenth century by Johann Gutenberg had been persistently opposed by governments; that the curbing of public communications had been so extensive that for 200 years printing in Europe could be likened to Rousseau's mankind, "born free, but everywhere in chains." In making their own revolution, they felt themselves moving in the spirit of John Milton's *Areopagitica:*

> Give me the liberty to know, to utter, and to argue freely according to conscience, above all liberties. . . . Though all the winds of doctrine were let loose to play upon the earth, so Truth be in the field, we do injuriously, by licensing and prohibiting to misdoubt her strength. Let her and Falsehood grapple; whoever knew Truth put to the worse in a free and open encounter.

Areopagitica had been the core of the Zenger defense in 1735. Benjamin Franklin was one of many colonists to support the immigrant printer, whose New York *Weekly Journal* had fulminated against William Cosby, the profligate royal governor. Franklin had helped persuade Andrew Hamilton to plead Zenger's cause. Hamilton's defense was Miltonian, declaring that "the words themselves must be libelous—that is, false, scandalous and seditious, or we are not guilty." Hamilton claimed "a right—the liberty—both of exposing and opposing arbitrary power by speaking and writing truth." The verdict upholding Zenger became part of the tradition which was to make the Constitution as originally drafted unacceptable without the Bill of Rights.

The First Amendment was all encompassing:

> Congress shall make no law respecting an establishment of religion, or prohibiting the free exercise thereof: or abridging the freedom of speech, or of the press. . . .

4

The founders recognized journalism as a restless, cantankerous force. At the time, the nation's fledgling press was tendentious, wildly partisan and, all too often, wilfully and grossly inaccurate. Although Jefferson once wrote "Nothing can now be believed which is seen in a newspaper," he never recanted another statement upholding the right of a free press. As he put it:

> The basis of our government being the opinion of the people, the very first object should be to keep that right; and were it left to me to decide whether we should have a government without newspapers or newspapers without government, I should not hesitate a moment to prefer the latter. But I mean that every man should receive these papers, and be capable of reading them.

Many in the young Republic did not agree with Jefferson. Some refused to tolerate the waywardness of editors. When George Washington was vilified in the press, notably by Franklin's grandson in the Philadelphia *Aurora,* it was wrecked by an angry mob. The ill-advised and hastily passed Alien and Sedition Acts of 1798 were turned against editors and many were charged with "writing and printing false, scandalous and malicious" statements against the government and the congress. Jefferson, after taking office as President, stopped further prosecutions.

Yet through much of the nation's history, the press has continued to be a troublesome presence. Frequently, the press has been irresponsible; always it has been a constant and visible target. Newspapers were wrecked by mobs on both sides of the slavery-abolitionist battle preceding the Civil War; one such mob martyred the Illinois abolitionist editor, Elijah P. Lovejoy. During the Civil War, generals like Burnside and Dix used their powers to suppress newspapers in Chicago and New York. In World War I and after, superpatriots sought to punish editors of whom they disapproved through the Espionage Act of 1917. Later, there were other and different attacks. In the 1930s, Huey Long of Louisiana, for instance, induced a compliant legislature to place a tax on advertising; it was struck down by the courts as "a deliberate and calculated device to limit the circulation of information." During the 1940s, some judges in Southern and

Western states sought to impose contempt citations on editors who insisted on appraising the operations of their courts. And throughout our history, the chief executive and other government officials have found reason to deplore, scold or denounce one or another segment of the press, including the minority press.

This continuity of conflict makes clear that friction is inevitable between a free press and government, and that it is most strained when the public is deeply divided over issues. So it was inevitable that controversy over governmental power and freedom of the press should erupt in the current climate of opinion, a climate formed in part by the unprecedented crises that the nation has been experiencing since the holocaust of World War II and its Cold War aftermath. Now the nation is contending with deep divisions—between a younger generation which accuses its elders of enshrining materialism, practicing materialism, and contaminating the atmosphere; between minorities who charge their fellow citizens with racist tendencies that bar the way to equal opportunity; between rich and poor, the citydweller and the suburbanite, the hawks and the doves.

The nation's press reflects these divisions. Its coverage is frequently apocalyptic; dwelling on crime, drugs, violence, corruption, welfare scandals, pollution, financial crisis—and the prolonged war in Indochina. It should come as no surprise that there has been increasing hostility and a widening credibility gap between the government and the press and between the press and the public. Unquestionably the media are not blameless. On the contrary, over the years their irresponsible scrambling for reader and viewer attention has only led many to look with skepticism at what they see on their television screens and to doubt what they read in their papers. Unfortunately, Vice President Spiro T. Agnew's criticisms, which created so much perturbation in the media and received so much approbation among sections of the public, have not helped matters. On the contrary, his attacks increased the acrimony and suspicion. In the last few years, news organizations have protested the issuance of subpoenas by federal grand juries ordering newsmen to testify and to produce notes, tapes, films, financial records, and other data sought by federal prosecutors in their investigations of left-wing militants and Black Panthers. Complaints were made that government agents were posing as newsmen to gather information on radical groups. It was in this troubled atmosphere that the Twentieth Century Fund assembled an independent Task Force on Governmental Power and Press Freedom, made up of jurists, lawyers and journalists.

Originally, we had intended to confine our study to the questions of subpoenas, law-enforcement agents posing as newsmen, official harassment of the so-called underground press and the government's criticisms—and investigations—of news judgments. But in the midst of our deliberations, we were confronted with the latest and most celebrated clash between government and press: the publishing of the Pentagon Papers and the attempts by the Nixon Administration to halt further publication. This collision, in which the right of the press to publish the classified material was upheld by the Supreme Court, is treated in a separate section of this report.

*   *   *   *

In our discussions, which were frequently far-ranging and always spirited, the task force did not feel it necessary to dwell overlong on the critical linkages between democracy, which depends on an informed citizenry, and the press, which is the purveyor of information to the public. But we all were well aware that the public has the biggest stake of all in seeing to it that the nation's press is protected against governmental intrusion or pressure. It is a truism that the public gets the newspapers it deserves, but we feel that the public has a right to fuller and fairer information than it has been getting. If government officials have sometimes been irresponsible toward the press, it is our view that the press has not always been responsible toward the public it serves.

We are in agreement that the nation's press must exhibit greater balance in its news judgments and higher ethical standards from its practitioners. All too often, the performance of journalists, particularly in dealing with governmental affairs, has been marked by a lack of basic understanding, by easy acceptance of "handout" information and by a misdirected passion for the headline or scoop. It is the task force's belief that journalism must clear itself of James Reston's charge that "most American newspaper people are really more interested in dramatic spot news, the splashy story, than in anything else. They want to be in on the big blowout, no matter how silly, and would rather write about what happened than whether it made any sense."

There is another problem of "access," involving press-public relations rather than press-government relations. That is the problem of affording the public, i.e. the individual citizen or groups of citizens, access to the news media.

Ben H. Bagdikian has noted, "In a large, urbanized society, individual free speech doesn't guarantee access to the marketplace of ideas," and he cites the suggestion of Professor Jerome A. Barron of George Washington University Law School that the interpretation of the First Amendment be expanded "to include the right of the individual to have a fair chance at access to the press, with the courts or legislatures deciding what is fair." That would seem a rather ponderous, time-consuming and costly way for an individual to seek a forum; but it must be acknowledged that although the path to the press is open through letters-to-the-editor columns, it is a very narrow path. For the broadcast media it is practically a closed path for a multitude of reasons including libel considerations, physical accessibility and cost. Still, it is inherent in the First Amendment that free speech is not completely free if it cannot find a free forum. Ultimately, a situation could arise in which government saw reason to intervene to assure access to the press, at which point the question of freedom would pose new uncertainties.

The difficult task of governing—and communicating in—a pluralistic society calls for greater responsibility on the part of both public officials and newsmen. That responsibility must begin at local and state levels, where mutual trust should be the keystone for effective conduct of public affairs. Unfortunately, this is not always the case. School, housing, health, and zoning boards have often tended to conduct public business in private meetings; when subsequent reports in the press, not unnaturally, are presented as exposés, the consequence is angry exchanges between government and press that confuse and distort public understanding. The problem becomes even more sensitive when newsmen venture into investigations of crime. It is an open secret that most stories of civic corruption stem from public officials with private knowledge willing to direct newsmen to incriminating evidence. If there has been any single ethic in American journalism it is that newsmen are prepared to protect such confidential news sources, likening their responsibility to the relationship existing between the clergy and their parishioners, doctors and patients, lawyers and clients.

The task force has sought to resolve the difficult problems confronting newsmen who are subpoenaed in order to get them to divulge confidential information. Until very recently, newsmen have not thought in terms of requiring legal protection, largely because they have felt themselves covered by the First Amendment. But the Supreme Court has before it three cases rooted in government subpoena issues, and unless the Court's determinations are broader than now anticipated, a majority of the task force favors recommendations to prevent the compelled disclosure of confidences by newsmen that might reduce or impair the flow of information to the public.

The task force also dealt with the attempts by governmental bodies to delve into the editorial judgments of the media. We welcomed the action of the House of Representatives in refusing to cite for contempt the Columbia Broadcasting System and its chief executive for declining to produce unpublished film and other background material demanded by a House Commerce subcommittee in an effort to investigate charges that the network had used some material out of context in the documentary "The Selling of the Pentagon." As we see it, the government lacks the legal authority to question the editorial judgments of the media, including television, radio and the underground press, which, according to some observers, can trace its origins to Tom Paine's *Common Sense.*

In studying the issues raised by publication of the Pentagon Papers, the task force found that the press did not challenge the government's right to protect confidential information affecting the security of the nation, its military forces and its diplomatic negotiations. The record of the press throughout two great wars and the protracted Cold War has been remarkable in its voluntary observance of security regulations. To be sure, the extent of federal classification procedures has been a vexing one. The press, under the rallying cry of "The People's Right to Know," has often been restive under what it regards as a paper curtain of excessive suppression. The system, if it can be called that, has spawned the practice of declassification by "leak," which became the focal battle over the Pentagon Papers. In supporting the right of newspapers to publish the material, the courts held that the administration had failed to demonstrate damage to essential national security. As Associate Justice Potter Stewart noted in his decision, "when everything is classified, then nothing is classified, and the system becomes one to be disregarded by the cynical and careless and to be manipulated by those intent on self-protection or self-promotion."

Each of the subjects covered by our report is important for a free press and an informed public. Our recommendations are designed to strengthen the press in its essential task of providing the public with information and to preserve a healthy adversary relationship between the press and the government. In our view, the health of that relationship is bound to suffer if publishers and editors bow to economic or political pressures and restrain reporters from adequate investigation or if public officials restrict or interfere with journalists in the performance of their professional duties.

Summary of Findings and Recommendations

The members of the task force represent different disciplines and views. We did not reach unanimous agreement on all of the many complicated issues before us. (Dissents are listed in the text.) But we shared in common a concern about governmental infringements, actual or potential, on the nation's press, and held in common a faith in the value,of free press as a disseminator of information to the public. Because we believe that a free and responsible press is, as William Ernest Hocking put it, "inseparable from the general meaning of freedom in a modern state," and because we are convinced with Learned Hand that "right conclusions are more likely to be gathered out of a multitude of tongues than through any kind of authoritative solution," the independent Task Force on Governmental Power and Press Freedom makes the following recommendations:

Press Subpoenas

An adequate newsmen's privilege should be incorporated into the law to protect the flow of information through the press to the public.

Confidences and Press Photographs

— The privilege should apply to personal testimony and records of journalists and to records of news organizations that might lead to the disclosure of confidential sources or of other confidential information.

— The privilege should be available to all journalists, including personnel of the "underground," collegiate and minority press.

— The privilege should extend to testimony before grand juries, preliminary hearings, trials, administrative hearings, legislative investigations and other bodies having the power of contempt.

— The privilege should authorize journalists to withhold the identities of confidential sources, as well as information given in confidence, and notes, tapes and other records of confidential communications.

— If the privilege is to be qualified, the qualifications should be as narrow and specific as possible. This could be done by specifying that if newsmen possess information about particular violent crimes, such as murder or kidnapping, they may be compelled to testify.

— In civil trials the privilege should be limited so that journalists cannot invoke it in order to avoid being held accountable for defamatory publications.

— The privilege should shield news organizations from being compelled to furnish unpublished photographs or unused television films of events, including rallies, demonstrations and disturbances.

Secret Testimony

— The privilege should shield journalists from having to appear for questioning before grand juries or other secret investigative agencies to the following extent: that when a subpoenaed newsman can make a showing that his newsgathering capacity would be seriously damaged merely by his entry into the secrecy of the interrogation room, then the official who subpoenaed him should be required to demonstrate a compelling need for his testimony before the journalist could be required to appear.

Investigations of the Broadcast Media

The public's need—and the value of democracy—of the fullest possible information can be threatened by Congressional investigations of editorial judgments, as well as by the Federal Communications Commission's questioning of editorial content.

— Because of the threat to press freedom posed by such governmental investigative efforts as the attempt by the House Committee on Interstate and Foreign Commerce to subpoena unpublished material from the CBS documentary film "The Selling of the Pentagon," no arm of the government should attempt to use the subpoena power to obtain the unpublished material of newsmen—whether in the regulated broadcast media or not.

— Because similar threats to the rights of a fully informed public can be posed by the Federal Communications Commission's questioning of editorial content in determining whether to grant or revoke licenses, a group of experts in the law and in broadcast journalism should undertake a careful study of how best to reconcile the competing values of journalistic freedom and governmental regulation.

Police Posing as Journalists

— The chief officers of all law enforcement and other public agencies that seek intelligence about domestic groups—and particularly those agencies that have permitted their agents to pose as journalists—should publicly disapprove of these masquerades and should take steps to ensure that they do not happen in the future.

— Law enforcement agencies should abandon the practice of employing journalists as informants. As citizens, journalists may choose to volunteer information to the police, but the payment of any money by the police to a journalist—either for "expenses" or for services rendered—in connection with the disclosure of information is tantamount to infiltration of journalism by the police and should be stopped.

The Underground Press

— The underground press should be considered entitled to all legal and constitutional rights applicable to other elements of the press, and all actions by public officials that discriminate against the underground press by subjecting it to arrests, searches, seizures or other official acts of harassment or intimidation should be vigorously opposed by the "established" press.

— The professional associations of journalism should form legal defense funds to aid underground publications when they are subjected to unlawful pressures from government officials.

Findings

Press Subpoenas

The present tension between the press and government was brought into focus by a series of subpoenas that have been issued by federal and state prosecutors over the past two years in efforts to compel newsmen to disclose information obtained from confidential sources. These subpoenas have raised in the clearest form the central issue: that the government's law enforcement efforts—particularly those directed at political radicals—are taking forms that pose a serious threat to the confidence between journalists and their sources, thus reducing the free flow of information to the public. In some instances, journalists have been forced to be ready sources of evidence for the government, serving as an investigative arm of law enforcement.

In the matter of the press subpoenas, the issue has been brought swiftly before the United States Supreme Court. Three newsmen, Earl Caldwell of *The New York Times,* Paul M. Branzburg of the *Louisville Courier-Journal,* and Paul Pappas of WTEV-TV in New Bedford, Massachusetts, were subpoenaed and refused to testify. In each instance secret grand jury testimony was demanded. Mr. Caldwell and Mr. Pappas were called to testify about black radicals; Mr. Branzburg was to be questioned about alleged marijuana and hashish offenses. Each man asserted that to testify would destroy his confidential relationships with his sources and would impede the flow of information to the public. They contended that the First Amendment's free press guarantee thus shields them from having to comply with the subpoenas. The Supreme Court will hear arguments on the three cases during the 1972 Court term.

The Supreme Court's decisions in these cases will be its first regarding the protection, if any, extended by the First Amendment to journalists in the news-gathering process. Previous decisions by the Supreme Court have dealt solely with newsmen's rights to publish the news. Thus these forthcoming decisions are likely to go far toward determining the extent to which newsmen may be shielded by the Constitution from being compelled to testify about information received in confidence. Since the common law does not recognize a "newsman's privilege," if the Court should hold that the First Amendment grants little or no protection from subpoenas, then important public decisions will have to be made as to whether Congress and the state legislatures should pass "shield" laws to protect newsmen from being forced to disclose confidences.

The members of the task force state no opinion, of course, as to the First Amendment issues posed by the pending Supreme Court cases. But we agree that press subpoenas pose a threat to the free flow of information to the public. Some of us feel that the First Amendment covers the news-gathering process completely, constituting a "newsman's privilege" that shields journalists from being required to disclose confidences under any circumstances; those members who take this point of view argue against the enactment of "shield" statutes for fear that they would narrow constitutional privilege. Others feel that legislation is generally better suited than constitutional rulings to creating a complete and detailed newsman's privilege. But since the Supreme Court's forthcoming decisions may well determine whether newsmen's privilege is to be based on the First Amendment or on statutes, the task force has decided to confine its views to those details that will have to be considered, whether by judges or by legislators. It is hoped that these views of the task force will provide helpful insights to those who will eventually deal with this important problem of governmental power and press freedom.

Competing values of press freedom and law enforcement effectiveness will undoubtedly have to be resolved. Critics of a newsman's privilege argue that there is scant empirical proof that the lack of a privilege has a significant impact upon the flow of news. They say that many reporters can convince their sources that the journalists would go to jail before betraying a confidence. Moreover, critics suggest that many news sources want to get their views before the public and are willing to take the risk that their confidences might be disclosed.

In contrast, those who support the privilege claim that there is even less proof that law enforcement would be handicapped, other than in rare, extraordinary situations, if it could not subpoena newsmen. They point out that press subpoenas have usually been issued in two situations: when radical groups are being investigated and reporters are known to have some knowledge of the radicals' affairs; and when reporters have published articles publicizing the existence of consensual or "victimless" crimes, prosecutors may be tempted to use press subpoenas because evidence is difficult to obtain by other means.

The task force believes that the mere existence of legal controls over press subpoenas would discourage their use. In the year that has passed since Attorney General John N. Mitchell issued guidelines governing the subpoenaing of newsmen by Justice Department lawyers, only three such subpoenas have been issued—a marked decline over the previous year.

The subpoenas issued over the past two years reveal that the question of newsmen's privilege has become vastly more complicated than it appeared to be only a few years ago. Eighteen states now have "shield" laws establishing a newsman's privilege.* Although many of these laws were passed within the last decade, most are already obsolete because they protect journalists only

*A complete list of state "shield" laws is reproduced in the appendix.

from having to reveal the names of their sources. The current subpoena controversy has underscored the inadequacy of the law in most jurisdictions to protect the lines of communication from news sources to the public. The task force has concluded that legal reforms are needed in a number of areas to assure that the free flow of information is not curtailed.

1. **Defining the press: The task force recommends that the newsman's privilege be designed to shield the press as an institution in its efforts to gather and disseminate the news.** It should reach beyond daily newspapers to protect the periodical, minority, underground and collegiate press, the broadcast media, newsletter and news services. It also should extend beyond actual news-gatherers to cover editors and other supervisory personnel.

Surprisingly, some of the state newsman's privilege statutes fail to cover classes of journalists who often need protection most. Several of these laws do not cover the broadcast media. Some do not protect magazine writers. Even the broad New York "shield" law fails to cover the underground and the collegiate press.

Because any privilege can be expected to exact a price by limiting the truth-finding functions of the courts, **the task force believes that privilege should not be extended beyond the limits necessary to protect the regular flow of information to the public through the efforts of journalists.** Accordingly we are of the opinion that the newsman's privilege should cover only those persons engaged in gathering, writing, editing, producing and supervising the collection of information for dissemination in such media as newspapers, news services, newsletters, periodicals, radio and television.

2. **Privilege against being required to disclose confidential sources or information: The task force recommends, subject to qualifications discussed later, that when a reporter is subpoenaed to give testimony, he should have the right to withhold the identity of his sources, plus any information received in confidence and any information that will damage his confidential relationship.** It follows from this recommendation that his notes, tapes or other records of confidential communications should also be privileged.

We recognize that reporters may feel that they should testify and that they can do so without undermining press freedom and therefore recommend that the law should not preclude the posing of such questions to journalists, so that they can respond if they deem it appropriate to do so.

3. Privilege against being required to appear to testify: Some lawyers and journalists have argued that the reporter's privilege should not merely protect reporters from having to disclose confidential sources or confidential information, but that in some instances it should also shield them from having to testify about any matters in secret. This was the argument made by Earl Caldwell of *The New York Times.* He asserted that by merely entering the grand jury room, with its secret interrogation, he would appear to be cooperating with the government in its investigation of the Black Panthers. Such a step would seriously undermine his capacity to obtain information in the future, he contended, and would violate his First Amendment rights as a newsman. The United States Court of Appeals for the Ninth Circuit agreed. It held that "where it has been shown that the public's First Amendment right to be informed would be jeopardized by requiring a journalist to submit to secret grand jury interrogation, the government must respond by demonstrating a compelling need for the witnesses' presence before judicial process properly can issue to require attendance."

The Ninth Circuit noted that the district court had already held that Mr. Caldwell could not be forced to disclose confidential information unless the government could demonstrate "a compelling and overriding national interest in requiring Mr. Caldwell's testimony which cannot be served by any alternative means." As the Ninth Circuit saw it, this meant that Mr. Caldwell could not be required to tell the grand jury more than he had written in his article—an exercise that would probably be a waste of time for all concerned. It concluded that nothing would be lost to the government if it were required to make a showing of "compelling" need before even subpoenaing Mr. Caldwell to enter the grand jury room.

The task force recommends a broad newsman's privilege against journalists having to disclose confidential sources, or information received in confidence. Armed with this protection, newsmen should be subject to the normal subpoena power of grand juries, except in extraordinary circumstances. We state no opinion as to the First Amendment issue confronting the Supreme Court in the *Caldwell* case. But to legislatures considering creation of a reporter's privilege, the task force recommends that where a subpoenaed reporter can make a showing that his or her news-gathering capacity would be seriously damaged merely by entry into the secrecy of the grand jury room, then the prosecutor should be required to demonstrate a compelling need for the testimony before the journalist could be required to appear.*

4. Photographs and film: A particularly troublesome problem arises when the government seeks to subpoena unpublished still photographs or unused television film taken by news cameramen at public meetings, demonstrations or disturbances. In such situations there is not an orthodox confidential relationship, since participants at the event know that their pictures may be published. But it is also understood that the photographer is a neutral recorder. Photographers are not expected to serve as an investigative arm of the prosecution by supplying photographs of persons who were not included in the published or broadcast pictures. To force them to act as such through subpoenas would do more than breach this implied confidence—it would probably subject photographers to attacks from participants in such events, and would reduce the news photographers' ability to cover the news.

The courts have not yet had an opportunity to work out the proper limits of this aspect of the reporter's privilege. Some newspapers have refused to give the government more than glossy prints of photographs that were published; one has compromised by turning over other photographs of individuals who were identifiable in published pictures.

Whenever the issue has been raised, it has exposed deeply conflicting values. Prosecutors, believing that newspaper or television files may contain filmed proof of guilt in arson or riot cases, have sought to get that material. Defendants, hoping that newspaper,

* Bert Early dissents: see Notes on Task Force Report.

magazine and television films will prove their absence at riots, have also attempted to subpoena film from the media. Journalists, having no desire to protect any person who was photographed committing a crime but realizing that the media's role as observer will suffer if it becomes recognized as a ready source of evidence, have balked. Some publications and television stations have begun routinely to destroy film that might be subpoenaed—a strong indication of the need for a reasoned legal solution.

The task force's studies reveal that this problem usually arises in such circumstances as riots or demonstrations, in which photographers who are present at a public place to photograph actions by a group record activities that are subsequently alleged to have been unlawful. For example, prosecutors have sought to subpoena the photograph files of *The St. Louis Post-Dispatch* after the burning of an ROTC building following a demonstration on the campus of Washington University and to subpoena photographs taken by the University of Maryland's campus newspaper of a violent demonstration on the campus; California officers have made use of a search warrant in an attempt to seize incriminating photos of a student disturbance from the *Stanford Daily;* and officials in Washington, D.C., have tried to obtain photographs taken by Washington newspapers of destructive demonstrations at Howard University.

The task force believes that in situations such as these, news organizations should be privileged not to furnish any photographs or films beyond those that were published. Normally, the most descriptive pictures will be published by the media, and to make others available solely for the purpose of aiding one side or the other in a legal action would compromise the neutral position of the press.

It must be emphasized that the ultimate interest at stake is the public's access to information, not a possessive attitude by the news media toward its pictures. Obviously, the line of least resistance for the press would be to surrender the photographs. But journalists know that if they become a ready source of court evidence news photographers will lose the free access to events that they now usually enjoy—and that if such access is lost, it is the public's view of news events that will suffer.*

5. **Records of news organizations:** Sometimes records of a newspaper or television network's telephone calls, disbursements, expense accounts or other records can disclose the identity of a source as unerringly as the compelled testimony of a reporter. There have been instances in recent months in which prosecutors have attempted to subpoena such records. **The task force recommends that when a news organization can show that a subpoena calls for documents or other evidence that would disclose confidential sources or information, then the subpoenaed organization should be privileged not to produce them.**

6. **Qualifications:** Some of the state shield laws create an unqualified journalist's privilege. Others qualify the privilege in one of two ways: (a) by declaring that a judge may divest a journalist of the privilege and order him to testify under certain general circumstances, such as "to prevent a miscarriage of justice," or "to protect the public interest"; or (b) by stating that in investigations of certain crimes, such as murder, kidnapping, or those that pose "a threat to human life," the privilege is revoked.

The theory behind these qualifications is that society will benefit more from obtaining information in exigent circumstances than from protecting journalistic confidences. Appealing claims can be made for qualifying the reporter's privilege to allow for such exigencies. It is difficult to argue that a reporter should be permitted to stand mute in, say, a kidnap case when a child's life is at stake. Yet any reporter's privilege will be weakened to the extent that it can be waived and it is possible that such exceptions can swallow the rule—that is, the privilege can be so easily divested that news sources will have no assurance that their confidences will actually be protected by the law.

A majority of the task force believes that, as a practical matter, no "safety valve" qualifications are needed.† A journalist is rarely given information about a grave criminal offense; but when he is, the information is usually published. In the even rarer event

---

* Roger Rook and Ralph de Toledano dissent; see Notes on Task Force Report.
† Judge Robert Williamson and Mr. Early dissent.

that a journalist receives such information and believes so strongly in the need for confidentiality that he neither publishes it nor volunteers it to the police, it is doubtful that he would divulge it under any circumstances. This reasoning about the practicalities of the reporter's privilege seems to have been borne out in practice. In states with statutes that do not qualify the privilege it has encountered no major objections. The New York State Legislature, which recently had a careful study of the problem done before enacting a detailed shield statute, did not qualify the privilege.

Although most task force members saw no need for safety valves, they acknowledged that there are some strong arguments in favor of qualification. All of us believe that if the privilege is to be qualified, the qualifications should be as narrow as possible. But a majority of the task force does not favor the general "public interest" qualification. The application of such a qualification usually comes at a time of great public concern over a newsman's refusal to testify about such emotionally charged and politically sensitive subjects as the narcotics trade or corruption of public officials. Under these circumstances the pressures will always be strong for the trial judge to conclude that it would be in the public interest for the journalist to testify.

Accordingly, a majority of the task force recommends that if there are qualifications, they must be stated as precisely as possible in the statute, so that the reporter and his or her source can know, at the time when confidential information is passed, whether the journalist will be protected by the shield law from having to identify sources. This qualification might be achieved by specifying in the law that if reporters have information concerning particular heinous crimes, such as murder or kidnapping, they may be compelled to testify.

7. Where the privilege should apply: The task force believes that the privilege for newsmen and -women should apply before grand juries, preliminary hearings, criminal trials, administrative hearings, legislative investigations and other official bodies that have contempt levying power to compel testimony. Civil suits raise special considerations of press freedom and responsibility, but they do not involve similar problems of conflicting public interests. Yet American society seems to be entering a phase of increased interest in corporate responsibility and consumer rights. Journalistic muckraking into corporate and business affairs is on the rise. We recommend that some form of journalist's privilege be observed in civil litigation, in order to keep open the avenues of information about corporate affairs. If exceptions are required, they must be drawn so that reporters cannot use the privilege improperly when they or their publication are defendants in a civil suit for libel or violation of privacy. This limitation is especially required when the plaintiff is faced with a First Amendment burden that prevents him from winning his suit unless he can show that the newspaper printed a false and defamatory story without making an adequate effort to check the facts. Assuming that a broad journalist's privilege will be recognized by the courts or legislatures, rules will have to be worked out to lift the privilege when a journalist-defendant invokes it to shield his own failure to check the facts adequately.

Investigations of the Broadcast Media

An essential corollary of the principle of press freedom is broad protection. To insist on the First Amendment rights of newspapers and magazines but not of the electronic media invites governmental encroachment on all forms of news gathering and dissemination. For if government acts as arbiter over the editorial affairs of the electronic media, controlling them in the guise of "legislative oversight" or regulations of the Federal Communications Commission, then a principle has been established which may eventually be applied to other forms of free expression.

There is, of course, some justification for government's involvement in the editorial affairs of television and radio. Anyone with sufficient determination and capital can publish a newspaper, but only so many channels are available to television, and these by right belong to the public. The allocation of these channels must therefore pass through the Congress and the FCC.

The task force recognizes that this regulatory obligation

creates serious conflicts between the "public interest" and the First Amendment. The nature of the "public interest," after all, is difficult to define, which means that government must tread very lightly, if it treads at all. There is no disputing its right to intervene against fraudulent or misleading advertising.

Regulation of television content is a problem because it is the nation's major—or most popular—source of news and news commentary. The television documentary, moreover, has become an important addition to the news process. It is assumed the networks, as well as individual stations, operating under public sufferance, are impartial in dealing with controversial issues. But a growing number of persons believe television has sometimes permitted its reporters, writers and producers to slant the truth while presenting the news.

Does this belief warrant governmental interference in the editorial process? Does the obvious fact that the television viewer cannot take his trade elsewhere give the Congress and the FCC the right to impose punitive measures on television when, in their judgment, television exceeds the bounds of editorial probity? These are difficult questions; they become manageable only if the concept of freedom of expression remains paramount.

These strictures can be but cold comfort for the television industry. Television stations are faced with winning renewal of their licenses every three years. If, for one reason or another, they invite the displeasure of groups which can gain the ear of the FCC, they are faced with a possibility of a loss of license. Worse still, a network can be brought before a Congressional committee to explain its editorial judgments on pain of a contempt citation if it refuses to lend itself to editorial second-guessing, which was the experience of CBS News with its documentary, "The Selling of the Pentagon."

There is very little dispute over the facts in the case. On February 23, 1971, CBS News broadcast a documentary on the activities of the Defense Department. Its thesis was that the Pentagon spent millions of the taxpayers' dollars in an effort to sell its military programs. "The Selling of the Pentagon" was praised by some as a contribution to the public's knowledge of military chicanery, but drew criticism for being misleading and heavily slanted from others.

The task force believes the merits or demerits of the broadcast are irrelevant as is the evidence that CBS edited interviews of at least two Pentagon officials in a manner which led to charges of deception. In one instance, a statement of Assistant Secretary of Defense Daniel Z. Henkin in answer to a question from a CBS interviewer was attached to the response of a subsequent question. In another, a quotation from a speech by Colonel John A. Mac-Neil was made to appear as if he were expressing his own views. According to the complete text of his statement, he was quoting another person, though he seemed to agree with the views he was quoting.

The result was an outcry from certain members of Congress demanding an investigation of CBS. Chairman Harley O. Staggers of the House Committee on Interstate and Foreign Commerce, which has legislative jurisdiction over the FCC and the radio-television industry, scheduled an investigation, and on May 26, 1971, a subpoena was served on Dr. Frank Stanton, president of CBS. The subpoena directed him to submit "all film, workprints, outtakes, and sound-tape recordings, written scripts and/or transcripts utilized in whole or in part by CBS in connection with" the documentary.

Dr. Stanton appeared before the Staggers Committee but refused to produce the materials demanded of him. "If newsmen are told that their notes, films, and tapes will be subject to compulsory process so that the government can determine whether the news has been satisfactorily edited, the scope, nature, and vigor of their news gathering and reporting will inevitably be curtailed," Dr. Stanton said. He insisted that no committee of the Congress has the power to "engage in official surveillance of journalistic judgments" by investigating particular news reports for distortion.

Representative Staggers replied that the subpoena was a proper exercise of his committee's supervision of the television industry. The broadcast media have the capacity to change and manipulate the recorded statements of individuals, he added, so that legislation might be required to prevent deceptive news editing. He went on to argue that both the public and those filmed by CBS have First Amendment rights equal to those of the television medium. When Dr. Stanton still refused, the committee voted to recommend that CBS and Dr. Stanton be cited for contempt of Congress. In a rare refusal of the House to support such action by one of its committees, the contempt citation was voted down.

It is the position of the task force that this retreat from the committee recommendation, while commendable, left the question of governmental intrusion into television's editorial process up in the air. Representative Staggers and a majority of his committee still apparently believe that their mandate to regulate the radio and television industries gives them the right to employ the subpoena power to second-guess journalistic judgments of the broadcast news media. As the task force sees it, this view ignores a critical distinction between the government's power to prevent deception on quiz shows and commercial advertisements and its responsibility, if any, to supervise the quality and accuracy of news. The difference is the First Amendment.

The task force believes that Congress has no more power to subpoena the files of a broadcast news organization in an effort to investigate its journalistic judgments than it has to subpoena the editorial files of a newspaper for the same purpose. Precisely because the broadcast media *do* exist under governmental regulation, there are strong reasons why this principle should be firmly established.

It is important to recognize the distinction between the constitutional validity of a press subpoena issued for the purpose of investigating a journalistic decision, and a subpoena issued in the course of an investigation of events outside the realm of journalism. An example of the latter is the Earl Caldwell case. His unpublished material was sought in connection with an investigation of alleged crimes by Black Panthers. The Supreme Court has yet to say to what extent, if any, the First Amendment protects a journalist's unpublished materials from such subpoenas. There is considerable doubt that a subpoena is valid when it is issued to obtain information for a governmental inquiry into the handling of unpublished material itself.

Because the government has the power to withdraw a radio or television station's license, journalists in the broadcast media may be particularly susceptible to the "chilling" effect of governmental second-guessing of their work. In the event that their materials were subject to subpoena, they would be under strong pressure to trim their sails when criticizing the government. For if a strong news item might provoke an investigation, and the government had the power to subpoena the "out-takes" from a television film or the words omitted from the final draft of a news comment, some fault might be found with their editorial judgments. Station licenses—and jobs—could be at stake, so that radio and television journalists would be working under an inhibiting burden. Whenever an editorial decision required subtle and delicate balancing of various considerations, the journalist would be aware that some official or Congressman, who might be offended by the article, might make a public issue of the editing—with the station's license perhaps at stake. Such a condition would lead to curtailment of robust reporting of controversial issues affecting the government—precisely what the First Amendment seeks to prevent. The task force believes, therefore, that no arm of the government has the legal authority to issue a subpoena for a reporter's unpublished material.

The task force realizes that the relationship of radio-television to government is a highly complex one, and that to insist that broadcast journalists' unused materials be given the same constitutional protection as the notes of newspapermen and -women does not resolve all the tensions between government regulation and free expression. Under a regulatory system a radio or television station can lose its license because of the editorial content of its news and public service broadcasts, which poses a threat of subtle governmental control and self-censorship discouraging bold and forceful expression. Yet we recognize that it is not tenable to assert that a licensee of one of the limited number of broadcast channels should be permitted to use its monopoly of that channel to discredit, malign or ignore groups in the community.

To resolve the conflict between these competing values of journalistic freedom and governmental regulation is an issue of great importance and extreme difficulty, one that is beyond the scope of this study and the expertise of this task force. The task force urges that a group of experts experienced in the law and the broadcast media undertake a careful study of these problems.

Police Posing as Journalists

In recent months a series of unrelated and apparently uncoordinated instances have come to light in which personnel of government intelligence and law enforcement agencies have posed as news reporters or photographers. In a variation of this practice, law enforcement agencies have paid reporters and press to obtain material for governmental use. These incidents appear to be regrettably widespread, both geographically and organizationally. They have occurred from Washington to Saigon and within the Army, the Federal Bureau of Investigation and local police forces.

Whether such incidents were common in the past and were undiscovered is not known. But it does seem significant that a rash of these occurrences has come to light within the past two years, almost in rhythm with the rising tempo of dissent, violence and official concern about political protest and violence. In fact, most of the instances that have been discovered involved police investigations of political dissenters—groups about which the public should be as fully informed as possible. However, the frequency with which police have been found to be posing as newsmen has tended to raise barriers of suspicion that have made it more difficult for the press to cover many events.

The limited time and investigative means at the disposal of the task force did not permit exhaustive verification of all incidents that were brought to its attention. But we have verified that at least fourteen such events have occurred:

— In Saigon, in 1969, two U.S. agents were found to have infiltrated the press corps.

— The Army Security Agency painted a van with the name of a non-existent television company and filmed demonstrators at the Democratic National Convention in 1968.

— Army intelligence agents also posed as TV cameramen during the Presidential Inauguration activities in Washington in January 1969.

— In July 1970, a female intelligence agent for the District of Columbia police department posed as a reporter to gain access to a welfare-rights group's meeting.

— Army intelligence agents obtained press credentials from the New York City Police Department to cover actions of H. Rap Brown and Stokely Carmichael in New York during the summer riots of 1967.

— In Wichita, Kansas, press credentials were given to local policemen during a visit by Vice President Agnew in October 1970.

— A member of the Chicago Police Department's Intelligence Division was discovered in March 1971 posing as a newsman to gain information from black students at a protest rally.

— Two plainclothes officers of the Nassau County, N.Y., police force posed as photographers for a weekly newspaper in order to photograph the audience at a veterans' antiwar rally.

— An Army agent masqueraded as a reporter for the *Richmond Times Dispatch* to obtain information on the Southern Christian Leadership Conference.

— A Detroit policeman posed as a news photographer to observe a General Motors stockholders' meeting in May 1970.

— In Albuquerque a city policeman posed as an Associated Press photographer at the University of New Mexico campus during demonstrations protesting the invasion of Cambodia in the spring of 1970.

— Complaints by newsmen covering July 4, 1971, ceremonies in San Juan, Puerto Rico, that police were posing as reporters led to an admission by the Commonwealth Secretary that his department had been issuing press credentials to police for about eight years.

— At a draft-card burning demonstration outside the Supreme Court in June of 1968, reporters for the *Washington Post* and *Boston Globe* spotted, along with the familiar faces of the Washington press, men whom they recognized as F.B.I. agents using television cameras and tape recorders to interview the demonstrators.*

— In the spring of 1971, a man recognized as an F.B.I. agent by Pulitzer Prize-winning reporter Jack Nelson of the *Los Angeles Times* was observed taking notes with reporters at a meeting called by Congressman William R. Anderson of Tennessee to discuss the Berrigan conspiracy prosecution. The man denied he was an F.B.I. agent, insisting that he was a writer; but he ran away when asked by a Congressional aide to identify himself. The aide followed the man outside the building and saw him enter a car. *Life* magazine reported a check of the license plates later traced the car to the F.B.I.

All but one of these incidents involved police or intelligence agents masquerading as journalists to gather information about dissident groups or to investigate other "political" matters. The reason seems obvious: law enforcement agencies tend to be ill-informed about political dissenters who do not fit the traditional "criminal" mold, and reporters often have easy access to them. However, when policemen masquerade as reporters, the same kind of forces come into play that arise when journalists are subpoenaed, except that the effect is more direct. As in the subpoena situation, the target groups are usually highly suspicious of officialdom and "establishment" institutions and are likely to freeze the press out at any indication that the media are serving

* These incidents are documented and discussed in fuller detail in the background paper below.

law enforcement. This suspiciousness is compounded when the dissenters have good reason to believe that the "journalist" or "news cameraman" who takes such interest in their activities may very well be reporting to City Hall rather than to the city desk. The task force considers that the hostility and distrust demonstrated by some radical groups toward the press is due, at least in part, to such practices on the part of the police. Journalists have been assaulted by militants and excluded from their meetings, but the most serious threat posed by these police tactics is to the public. It cannot be fully informed of developments within all elements of our society if law enforcement authorities resort to masquerading and subornation. The principal reason why they should be stopped is not that they make the reporter's job more difficult, but that they may on occasion make the job impossible.

It seems likely that the increased use of such tactics will rapidly dissipate their usefulness to the police. As such incidents come to public notice, people will become reluctant to give important information to "reporters" not known to them; as reporters are increasingly frozen out of dissenters' meetings, so will the masquerading police agents be. In the end, law enforcement as well as the public will be shorter on information than before.

The task force condemns this form of masquerading by the police. It endangers the integrity of the press and renders it less effective in performing its responsibilities to society.

The task force notes that police officials in New York City, Chicago, Detroit and the District of Columbia have issued orders condemning the practice of police agents posing as newsmen. The Defense Department has issued an order that "there shall be no covert or otherwise deceptive surveillance or penetration of civilian organization unless specifically authorized by the Secretary of Defense or his designee." This order is regarded by Pentagon officials as prohibiting agents from posing as journalists.

In response to an inquiry from this task force, F.B.I. Director J. Edgar Hoover replied in a letter, "F.B.I. agents are not permitted to pose as reporters or press photographers in the course of their investigations."*

*Letter on June 7, 1971.

The task force is also concerned with a related practice in which the F.B.I. has been involved—compensating journalists for "services and expenses" involved in information-gathering. During the riot-conspiracy trial of the "Chicago Seven," in 1969, two journalists—Louis Salzberg and Carl Gilman—testified for the prosecution and said they had been paid for years as informants for the F.B.I. Mr. Salzberg, a photographer who began his connections with radicals as a staff member for a Spanish-language newspaper, acknowledged at the time that his F.B.I. salary had been $600 a month for at least one year. Mr. Gilman, a television newsman from San Diego, received about $10,000 for pay and expenses over a two-year period. Neither of the men was recruited by the F.B.I., but both began receiving compensation after they initiated the arrangements.

When the task force inquired of the Justice Department about the use of journalists as informants, John W. Hushen, Director of Public Information, sent the following reply "prepared by Director Hoover":

> The FBI accepts from any person information which may be of value in the course of an FBI investigation. The FBI does not now, and never has, actively recruited journalists as informants. However, there is no policy against accepting information from a journalist or any news media representative if it is volunteered, which was the case with Mr. Louis Salzberg and Mr. Carl Gilman. Both of these individuals furnished information to the FBI on a voluntary basis. They were paid for their services and expenses.*

While it is true the arrangements in these cases were initiated by the newsmen, the task force cannot accept the characterization of "volunteering" information as an act of citizenship, when the informant, be he a journalist or any other citizen, is paid.

When journalists are paid for providing information to the F.B.I. or any other law enforcement agency, the result is an infiltration—and sullying—of the profession. The task force concludes that the practice is damaging to press independence and

*Letter on June 7, 1971.

is wrong. We think that the same considerations that prompted Mr. Hoover not to permit his agents to pose as journalists should preclude the F.B.I. from accepting journalists as paid informants. The task force also believes that the practice of journalists accepting compensation for providing information is professionally unethical. We believe that a journalist who accepts any compensation for providing information or conducting surveillance for law enforcement officials—during work hours or not—has compromised his own neutrality as a journalist and has damaged the integrity of the journalist's craft.*

The Underground Press

The journalistic form that is generally known as the "underground press," "the radical press," "the alternative press," and by other names, has been a continual source of controversy in the matter of governmental power versus press freedom. Just as this form of journalism lacks a universally accepted name, so does it defy a precise definition. It has been described by one author as "a wildly unpredictable happening," as a journalistic expression of "abiding bitterness about the State of the Union," and by others as pornographic trash. In quantitative terms, it embraces 300 to 350 newspapers sprinkled across the country, plus about 200 additional publications that appear sporadically or in mimeographed form. They share a style that is irreverent, tolerant of some drugs, explicit about sex, oriented toward the political left, and consistently anti-establishment.

Its anti-establishment tone is significant, for underground publications are almost always out of favor with the local governments and in bad odor with other influential circles of the communities where they are published. They have greater proclivity for antagonizing officialdom than the daily press, yet have little or none of the protective political power of the established press. As the friction between militants of the left and the government has increased in the past few years, so have the occasions upon

---

* Mr. de Toledano dissents, Mr. Rook comments; see Notes on Task Force Report.

which local law enforcement officials have been outraged by statements in the underground press.

— In 1969 the publisher of the *Los Angeles Free Press* was fined $1,000 and placed on probation for three years for having published a purloined list of state narcotics agents.

— Dallas police raided an underground newspaper in October 1968 and hauled away two tons of material from an underground newspaper in an "obscenity" raid—yet failed to obtain an obscenity conviction that would stand up in Federal Court.

— The Police Department of Buffalo, New York, drove the Black Panther newspaper from the streets in August 1970 by announcing its intention to arrest any vendors selling the publication.

— Officials in Los Angeles, Philadelphia, Providence and Richmond denied press credentials to the reporters of the local underground newspapers.

— During the autumn of 1969, the San Diego *Street Journal's* office was searched by police without a warrant and its street vendors handcuffed, searched and jailed for loitering and obstructing the sidewalk.

There have been numerous other allegations by the underground press of heavy-handed treatment by law enforcement officials. *Orpheus,* a bimonthly publication of articles drawn from various underground newspapers, described the situation:

> Although these papers have been evicted from their offices and homes, harassed by the police, had their street sellers arrested en masse, had their benefit parties raided, been bombed, burned, beaten, gypped, framed and lost printer after printer, the underground press continues to increase in size and number.

The task force has listed only those incidents that have been verified in sworn court testimony or reported in the established press, but that is evidence enough to indicate that some law enforcement officials have used their official authority against the underground press in a way in which it would never have been invoked against the established press. These actions seem to have been based on the erroneous assumption that underground publications forfeit some degree of their protection under the First Amendment when they violate public standards of taste, preach a tolerance of drugs and sex, and criticize the police. There has been a double standard of treatment, one for the underground and one for the established press—a double standard that is inconsistent with the First Amendment's guarantee of freedom for all the press.

Unfortunately, the attitude of the established press toward official harassment of the underground press has been characterized by neglect. Of the numerous instances that were brought to the attention of the task force, instances in which elements of the underground press protested that they had been abused by the police, a majority were not mentioned in either the news or editorial columns of the established press. In those incidents that have developed into court cases, the underground press has been left largely to its own fragile devices by the more affluent elements of the news media. Others in the journalistic profession stood by and gave no aid in three legal actions involving the underground press that produced legal precedents damaging to all journalists—the prosecution of the *Los Angeles Free Press* for theft in 1969, the subpoenaing of the editor of the *Madison Kaleidoscope* after the bombing at the University of Wisconsin in 1970, and the denial of press credentials to the *Los Angeles Free Press* reporters in 1967.

The task force believes the underground press should be entitled to all legal and constitutional rights applicable to other sectors of the press, and all actions by public officials that discriminate against the underground press by subjecting it to arrest, searches, seizures or other official acts of harassment and intimidation should be vigorously opposed by all the press.*

In addition we recommend that journalism's professional associations form legal defense funds for the aid of underground publications subjected to unlawful pressures from government officials.

* Mr. Rook comments in Notes on Task Force Report.

The Pentagon Papers

A fundamental problem of the relationship between governmental power and the press was posed unexpectedly in June of 1971 when *The New York Times,* the *Washington Post* and other newspapers published what have become known as the Pentagon Papers—a group of documents compiled from Defense Department files for a study of the origins of American participation in the Vietnamese war.

The circumstances that surrounded the publication challenged many concepts of the security classification system with which the United States has lived, however uneasily, for a number of decades. The study itself, which had been ordered by Robert S. McNamara while Secretary of Defense, was classified Top Secret. There had been no authorization by any responsible government official for its release to the press. Many of the individual documents, consisting to a great extent of memoranda produced by high officials in the early sixties, were quoted directly by the newspapers without any effort to paraphrase and "fuzz over" their nature. Finally, the sheer bulk of classified material—some 7,000 pages—invited a governmental response. Officialdom could not ignore the papers as it customarily ignores leaks of individual bits of classified information from Washington.

Initially, the government reaction was to seek injunctions in the Federal courts against further publication of the documents, which were being released in serial form. For the purposes of this report, it is unnecessary to trace the various steps of the litigation.* The important fact is that on June 30, 1971, the Supreme Court of the United States, by a vote of six to three, dissolved injunctions by lower courts, permitting the newspapers to resume publication.

Even though it decided the case, the Court's decision did not resolve the conflict. The Justices were divided even more deeply than the six to three decision indicated, and each member set forth his own views in separate statements. The Court majority concluded that the government did not have the right to prevent

*The complete statements of the Judiciary are printed in the appendix.

the publication of the specific documents in question. But the judicial door seemed pointedly held open for future prosecutions for *having published* the papers. It would be fair to sum up the decision as one which told the newspapers that they could publish a specific set of documents at their own risk.

For the press as well as for students of the problems of a free society, the outcome did not clarify, once and for all, the relationship between the press and the government. At the heart of the issue was the question of prepublication restraint—whether there are circumstances under which the government has the right to *prevent* publication. Journalists and commentators have generally assumed that the government has no such right, whatever may be the legal authority to prosecute after the fact for the publication of material offensive to the law. Very few cases have come up in the Federal courts bearing upon the issue, and in the Pentagon Papers case the government conceded there had been none which raised the problem in the context of national security.

It is worth noting the wide range of attitudes among the Supreme Court Justices on the issue of pre-publication restraint. According to the late Justice Black, "every moment's continuance of the injunctions against these newspapers amounts to a flagrant, indefensible, and continuing violation of the First Amendment"; but according to the late Justice Harlan, prohibiting prior restraints does not reach "to the point of preventing courts from maintaining the status quo long enough to act responsibly in matters of such national importance as those involved here."

To Justice Douglas the First Amendment left "no room for governmental restraint on the press." By contrast, Justice Blackmun argued that "the First Amendment, after all, is only one part of an entire Constitution. . . . Each provision of the Constitution is important, and I cannot subscribe to a doctrine of unlimited absolutism for the First Amendment at the cost of downgrading other provisions. . . . What is needed here is a weighing, upon properly developed standards, of the broad right of the press to print and of the very narrow right of the Government to prevent." Justice Brennan stated that the First Amendment "tolerates absolutely no prior judicial restraints of the press predicated upon surmise or conjuncture that untoward consequences may result," although he conceded that "there is a single, extremely narrow class of cases (when the nation is at war) in which the First Amendment's ban on prior judicial restraint may be overridden."

Justice White held that "prior restraints require an unusually heavy justification under the First Amendment," and concurred in the majority finding because he did not believe the Government had met the test. But Justice Stewart commented that "I am convinced that the Executive is correct with respect to some of the documents involved. But I cannot say that disclosure of any of them will surely result in direct, immediate, and irreparable damage to our Nation or its people. That being so, there can under the First Amendment be but one judicial resolution of the issues before us. I join the judgments of the Court." Justice Marshall noted that Congress has specifically declined to grant the type of authority that the Government sought, adding "It is not for this Court to fling itself into every breach perceived by some Government official nor is it for this Court to take on itself the burden of enacting law, especially law that Congress has refused to pass."

Chief Justice Burger, who dissented from the majority, agreed that there are constitutional limitations on prior restraint. He went on to say that "adherence to this basic constitutional principle, however, does not make this case a simple one. In this case, the imperative of a free and unfettered press comes into collision with another imperative, the effective functioning of a complex modern government and specifically the effective exercise of certain constitutional powers of the executive. Only those who view the First Amendment as an absolute in all circumstances—a view I respect, but reject—can find such a case as this to be simple or easy."

In sum, while basic issues were posed, basic issues were not resolved. The outcome should not be considered a criticism of the Supreme Court. There is good reason to believe that the ends of justice are frequently best served when decisions are made on the narrowest possible grounds, and that sweeping questions of policy are best determined in other arenas. But whatever merit there may be to this view, the fact remains that there is as yet no authoritative concept of whether publication boundaries exist.

The debate outside the courts over publication of the Pentagon Papers centered on questions that were largely irrelevant to the issue of prepublication restraint. Generally speaking, commentators concentrated on such matters as whether the papers proved deception of the public by the government; the propriety of publishing the documents and the vagaries of the classification system. It is probable that most of the public debate reflected attitudes on the war in Vietnam rather than attitudes on press freedom.

In retrospect, it is hardly surprising that the Supreme Court decided the case on relatively narrow grounds or that the public debate was largely irrelevant to the long-range issue affecting the press. Whatever may be the venerability of the doctrine of no prepublication restraint, the publication of the Pentagon Papers raised the issue in a new context which could not have been foreseen by those who wrote the First Amendment. But if the context is new, it does not necessarily invalidate the principles which have governed past conduct. What is clear is that a re-examination is in order. The circumstances of the case required that the litigation be settled within a few weeks, which was hardly an atmosphere conducive to re-examination of underlying issues. From this standpoint, the conduct of the Supreme Court was probably an exercise in wisdom in which the decision did no violence to traditional concepts of freedom of the press while the individual opinions left open the possibility of calmer assessment.

By and large, those who regard the doctrine of no prepublication restraint as absolute base their conviction upon the *Areopagitica*, the Zenger case, and the ultimately successful opposition to the Alien and Sedition Acts, although probably few people, including newspapermen and -women, are familiar with their historical significance. They are traditional symbols for those who advocate a totally unfettered press, and they possess significance regardless of their factual content.

Their significance is that they took place when the struggle for freedom was directed against governments which thought they had an inherent right to censor the press in order to prevent dissension. The nations of Western Europe had lived with the "divine right" concept of government for so many centuries that it was difficult to emancipate men from its implications even after the concept itself had been formally renounced. So it was an accepted and explicit doctrine at the time of both John Milton and John Peter Zenger (and was implicit in the Alien and Sedition Acts) that "wrong thinking" could be suppressed and that authorities were acting quite properly when they curtailed the publication of material which embarrassed them.

The public was eventually freed from the divine right concept so thoroughly (at least in the United States) that the doctrine of no prepublication restraint became deeply entrenched. If the government in June 1971 sought to suppress the publication of the Pentagon Papers on the grounds that their revelation represented heresy or embarrassment to individuals, its case would have been tossed out of court. No such accusation was made. The government's case rested upon the charge that publication would injure the nation's security and could interfere with vital foreign negotiations.

Since it was never publicly disclosed, the precise nature of the alleged injury to the national security is unclear. Nevertheless, the government was making a claim for injunctive relief on grounds which the government conceded have never been presented to the Federal courts in the past. The argument may have been old wine in a new bottle, although when the label states that the action sought is for the protection of the people of the country rather than for the protection of orthodoxy or individual members of the government, it is necessary to take another look.

Legal issues aside, it also is necessary to take into account the general background against which the government's action took place. For at least twenty-five years, the United States has regarded itself as being "at war," whether "hot" or "cold," with an alien ideology. A people who are "at war" have a tendency, rightly or wrongly, to regard the normal processes of democratic life as subordinate to the goal of victory. A plea that certain information must be suppressed to keep it from the hands of an "enemy" or to permit the formation of alliances for "survival" has a much higher degree of acceptability in such an atmosphere than it would in more placid or pacific times.

The psychology of war also fosters a trend of thought which is difficult for a group to discuss calmly. It is based upon the assumption that there are different categories of "rights"—some a matter of "survival" and others a form of "luxury." Under such an assumption, the rights granted to an individual have a tendency to wind up in the second category and those granted to the government in the first. This condition fosters a predilection for very strict enforcement of constitutional guarantees for individual right in times of serenity when such guarantees are not needed and for foregoing the "luxury" in times of stress.

This type of thinking is more likely to characterize popular debate than judicial confrontation, and no member of the Supreme Court voiced such thoughts in relation to the Pentagon Papers. But it is only one step removed to conclude that there are certain areas in which some constitutional rights are mutually exclusive, and, therefore, a choice must be made. This consideration *did* influence the thinking of some court members, most notably the Chief Justice when he contrasted the "imperative" of an unfettered press with the "imperative" of "effective functioning" of government. His coherent statement can fairly be said to represent the thinking of a large body of responsible men and women who do not regard themselves as in any way opposed to a free press or a free society. It deserves careful analysis.

At first glance, the statement appears unexceptionable. For at least three decades, the nation has accepted the concept that there are "secrets" which would injure the United States if they were revealed to a hostile world. Obviously, it is impossible to publish such secrets in the public press without disclosing them to an enemy. Therefore, the right of a free press is incompatible with government effectiveness, and one must yield to the other. Once this line of reasoning is established, there seems to be little else to discuss other than the effectiveness of individual systems for maintaining the necessary secrecy while permitting the maximum degree of press freedom possible under such conditions.

It is possible to buttress this line of thought with a number of hypothetical examples which touch off emotional responses that subordinate critical analysis. Usually, they take the form of questions: Would you permit a newspaper to publish the movements of troop ships when enemy submarines are lurking offshore? Would you permit a newspaper to publish codes that would enable an enemy to learn our battle orders? Would you permit newspapers to publish stories that would reveal our weak spots in time of war? Would you permit newspapers to publish our plans of attack and the forces we are going to use?

The short and simple answer is that these questions pose only hypothetical dangers. The practicalities are well illustrated by the system of voluntary censorship set up through government-press cooperation during World War II. Despite occasional slips, usually inadvertent, these voluntary arrangements were entirely adequate to serve military necessity.

But while the dangers inherent in press freedom are largely hypothetical, the threat that would be posed to press freedom by prepublication restraints is very real. Historical experience is available, because what we now regard as the "free press" emerged only after a long struggle against licensing. The nation's founders knew what they were doing when they wrote the First Amendment. They had learned through bitter experience that no man—no matter how well-intentioned—can be entrusted with the power of censorship.

It is apparent that the doctrine of prepublication restraint can be made effective only through the use of censorship. Usually, the kind of material to which the government objects is not published in serial form. The Pentagon Papers were something of an exception in this respect, and it is unlikely that this kind of exception will occur again. If the government is really worried about its secrets, such fears can be allayed only by inspecting newspaper editions before they hit the streets. Such a practice would open nightmarish prospects for our free institutions.

The "hit-the-panic-button" type of question described above

can be, and frequently is, used to discredit all of the safeguards for individual liberty built into the Constitution. We hear such rhetorical inquiries all the time:

"Would you permit a communist spy to go free just because of the Fifth Amendment?"

"Would you turn a rapist loose to harm women and children just because there were a few technical irregularities committed by the police when they arrested him?"

"Would you turn loose drug peddlers just because a policeman forgot to get a warrant before entering their flat?"

When these questions are analyzed without the distorting influence of emotion all they are really asking is whether people accused of committing a crime should be turned loose simply because their guilt cannot be technically and legally proven.

The type of reasoning implied in such questions was rejected by the framers of the Constitution. They knew that rights which are only partially safeguarded are not safeguarded at all, and that people who truly want freedom must be willing to suffer some unpleasant consequences.

Secrecy itself, moreover, involves a price and can have consequences fully as adverse as a breach of secrecy. It has become increasingly apparent that many Americans are losing confidence in governmental institutions at all levels of society. Citizens have become more interested in and more critical of the manner in which such elementary matters as zoning laws, tax assessments, the flotation of school-board bonds, the actions of city councils, and the activities of state legislatures and governments are handled. To some extent at least, this is because secrecy has become inherent in government operations, making it difficult for the average citizen to satisfy himself that his affairs are under competent and honest management.

Society must realize that any degree of secrecy entails social costs. It is up to our society to examine these costs and to determine whether they are too high to pay.

Governmental secrecy has a peculiar characteristic that stems from the absence of a known method of confining its exercise to limited areas on which reasonable persons can agree. Because classified security material cannot be examined by the public, the public cannot know whether only material essential to the nation's security is being classified. When people do not know, they tend to become suspicious. These suspicions may not assume a dangerous form when times are good and governmental policies are working well. But at the first setback—and setbacks are inevitable no matter how wise political leaders and their policies may be—the suspicions emerge as a hardened conviction that secrecy has been used to conceal blunders or even fraud and venality. At that point, the declassification and revelation of classified papers does little to restore confidence. An administration that has once resorted to unjustified secrecy can do little to assure a disaffected or skeptical electorate that it is coming clean.

A society without traditions of freedom can handle such disaffection by physical suppression. A free society is a different proposition altogether. Unity cannot be sustained by rifles and police. It requires the confidence of the electorate. Without that confidence, a free government becomes ineffective.

The cost of secrecy is not confined solely to the breeding of suspicion that the government is playing fast and loose with the public trust. It is also a device for cutting off the public debate through which the citizens of a nation prepare themselves for the consequences of great decisions which may mean considerable sacrifice. Nowhere is this better illustrated than in the Pentagon Papers.

The significance of the Pentagon Papers to historians is highly debatable. Whether they shed light on the entry of the United States as a military force into Vietnam is something that cannot, at this point, be determined. But they are unquestionably revealing in terms of the quality of discussion which governed that entry. The most notable characteristic of the passionate debate which was going on within governmental circles is that it took place virtually out of sight and earshot of the public. The American people had only the faintest inklings of the facts and the decisions which were to determine their destiny.

Furthermore, the debate was not conducted under circumstances which fostered calm judgment. Within the government itself, only a relative handful of people were privy to all the facts and options. Yet even this handful were conducting themselves under circumstances which violated all the rules of adversary discussion. They were in a position to write memoranda but could not be certain who would read them or what effect they would have. They did not confront contrary points of view in situations where they could find out what arguments they had to counter. They had no real chance to test their own thinking against others.

In this connection, the Pentagon Papers provide an ironic example of the ultimate futility of secrecy. The papers were put together as a result of Secretary McNamara's request for a study to assist future policy planners in avoiding mistakes made in Vietnam. Once the documents were assembled, fifteen copies were printed and locked up where it was highly unlikely that any future planners would even see them. It is difficult to regard this procedure as a satisfactory method for learning from history.

One function of public debate is to test ideas in the marketplace of thought. Another function is to prepare people psychologically for stormy days ahead. In regard to the Vietnamese war, neither function was carried out. On the contrary, all informed discussions took place under a "security" tent. This process left the public in the bewildering position of finding itself involved in a major conflict with no idea of how it got into it or what it was fighting for. Did the United States gain enough advantages from its policy of secrecy to justify the price paid in loss of public confidence? On balance, has the secrecy that was practiced strengthened or weakened the nation?

The members of the Supreme Court addressed themselves to the propriety of the specific classifications of the Pentagon Papers and to the rights of the government to seek injunctive relief. **The task force urges the nation to ponder a broader question—the wisdom of unchecked secrecy itself.**

The task force does not propose the abolition of the security classification system, although we favor a serious study of it by a disinterested group. We are well aware that government of any character will continue to practice secrecy—for good or for bad reasons—in many of its operations. Government officials are human beings, and humans generally assume they have a right to privacy in the conduct of their affairs. It is difficult to convince a person that he does NOT have that right simply because his affairs are in a public domain.

Excessive secrecy is inimical to a free society and should be combatted. But we doubt that a law by itself can guarantee public inspection of the conduct of public business. **The task force believes that an effective and essential instrument to achieve this end is a free and responsible press—free to investigate; free to interrogate; and free to publish.**

When we weigh the imperative of secrecy against the imperative of an effective government in a free society, we believe that the balance is more heavily weighted in favor of the latter.

Admittedly, a free press is a troublesome institution. It can be, and frequently is, arrogant, obnoxious, wrong-headed. We have no illusions as to its reluctance to correct its own faults. But none of its defects is so grave as to justify the abridgment of freedom. Liberty is far too precious to be abandoned out of fear of unpleasant consequences.

Basic to freedom is the right to publish. Obviously, this is a right which entails risks—as does every other right in a free society. The founding fathers did not present the Constitution as a document to ensure a painless world. They claimed that it would safeguard liberty, which they considered a fundamental objective.

The task force has neither seen nor heard persuasive evidence that a free press will bring about the downfall of our nation. That latter condition is much more likely to come about through efforts of overly zealous government officials to protect the public from knowledge of how the public's business is transacted.

But we have seen and heard persuasive evidence that a free government can be effective only when it has the confidence of its citizens. The free press is the most effective instrument known to sustain that confidence. Therefore, a majority of the task force urges that our leaders regard the doctrine of no prepublication restraint as absolute. No matter what the difficulties, that long-term result will be a stronger and more united nation.*

Conclusion

When we met for the first time, the members of the task force possessed a wide variety of backgrounds and views on the problems of governmental power and press freedom. But all of us had already concluded from our observations of recent public events that new and potentially corrosive frictions were rising between the news media and the government. At the conclusion of our deliberations, we could appraise with precision the extent of the threat to press freedom. However, we achieved a consensus that some degree of damage to press freedom is posed by each of the five subjects discussed in this report: press subpoenas, police posing as newsmen, official harassment of the underground press, governmental investigations in the regulated broadcast media, and attempted prior restraint of publication.

Moreover, we share a feeling that press freedom might be more fragile than is widely assumed—and that its role in American democracy is so crucial that the nation cannot afford to risk its erosion. The fundamental truth about the constitutionally protected status of the press is that it exists for the public, not the press. As the late Justice Hugo L. Black put it in his opinion in the Pentagon Papers case: "In the First Amendment the founding fathers gave the free press the protection it must have to fulfill its essential role in our democracy. . . . The press was protected so that it could bare the secrets of government and inform the people. Only a free and unrestrained press can effectively expose deception in government."

If this principle were widely understood and vigorously defended by the public, there would be little cause for concern in governmental rumblings against the press. To act against the press would then be viewed by the people as a thrust against them, and politicians would hesitate to do so.

---

*Judge Williams, Mr. Early and Mr. Rook dissent from this position. Mr. de Toledano comments in Notes on Task Force Report.

But the public's reaction to some recent events reveals that many people do not consider that press freedom includes the obligation to report truths that are repugnant to a critical government. Public-opinion polls disclose that the public's patience with such journalism is dangerously thin—that many, if not a majority, of the people believe that the press is being either irresponsible or unpatriotic when it publishes material that the government feels should not be made public.

At the same time a large segment of the public has come to have as many reservations about government as about the press, as witness all the talk about "credibility gaps." Furthermore, the feeling that government policies and political leaders are increasingly being "sold" to the public by one cosmetic technique or another has led to wariness and suspicion of those policies and leaders. Thus there is an ambivalent erosion of confidence in the institutions that are supposed to represent the public, making the media as much victims as reporters of news events. If the press reports dissent, it is held also to be the vehicle of dissent; yet if it does not report, it is not doing its constitutional duty to serve as the bulwark against arbitrary government. This exacerbates tensions between government and press.

The public must recognize, as the men and women who fought for the Bill of Rights recognized, that a free and independent press is vital to a free people. In the last analysis, the public has the most to lose from a whittling away of the safeguards that have, since the founding of the nation, preserved and protected the invaluable tradition of a free press. It is therefore incumbent on the media continually to reaffirm their role in a democracy and to resist any infringement by government on their constitutional rights. For this, the courts are always open. At the same time, the media must also adhere fully to their responsibility to be an open conduit of information to the public. It is this above all that will make the maintenance of a free press not a cherished cliché but the cornerstone of a free society.

Notes on Task Force Report

Privilege Against Being Required to Appear to Testify, p. 19.
Mr. Early comments:
The Supreme Court of the United States has, as of this writing, granted certiorari to the *United States v. Earl Caldwell*, no. 1114 October Term 1970. Accordingly, the high court will deliberate the very issue of whether a journalist may constitutionally refuse in any circumstances to enter a grand jury room. The task force could therefore decline to predict the outcome of that deliberation and thus also avoid any suggestion of an effort to influence the result. But the task force having chosen to speak at this time I wish to note that, as a lawyer, I have serious doubts as to the correctness of the opinion of the Ninth Circuit or, if correct, as to its likely extension to different circumstances.

Photographs and Film, p. 20.
Mr. Rook comments:
In my view, there are only a few situations where unpublished photos and unused television film need to be protected from legal process.
Mr. de Toledano comments:
I take strong exception to the extension of the privilege to unpublished photographs or unused films of events where there is no element of confidentiality. This compromises the doctrine we are promulgating in this report. If an event is public, the photographs or film footage taken in no way involve a confidential relationship between newsman and source. The "communication" is in no way privileged. To hold that law enforcement authorities may not examine this material, after due service of subpoena, is to advocate obstructionism in the legal process.

Police Posing as Journalists, p. 29.
Mr. Rook comments:
While I do not approve of the general practice of police posing as reporters, I foresee situations where there may be a practical necessity. I do not see this as being as great a problem as the majority of the task force. Also I feel journalists should have freedom to provide information to the dispute-deciding process.

Mr. de Toledano comments:

The onus is misplaced here and should be placed on newsmen who act as paid informants to law enforcement agencies. These agencies seek information however and wherever they can. One reason that they accept paid informers is an attitude prevalent among newsmen that it is somehow reprehensible to aid the law enforcement process on a voluntary basis. That attitude has filtered through to the pages of this section of the task force report. Strongly as I deplore the prostitution of the news process by government use of paid journalistic informers, I find it distressing that some newsmen should consider it debasing to give aid to the law when it needs it.

The Underground Press, p. 34.
Mr. Rook comments:

I believe the underground press is entitled to the same constitutional protection as the established press but I do not accept the inference of the recommendation that the underground press should have a superior position by not being subject, under the careful strictures of the law, to arrest, search or seizure.

The Pentagon Papers, p. 37.
Mr. de Toledano comments:

I do not dissent from the absolute position taken by the task force on prior restraint. But I do take exception to the implicit argument that runs through this section of the task force report—namely, that government secrecy is unnecessary and counter-productive, and that no harm was done by the publication of the Pentagon Papers. In delicate diplomatic maneuver, secrecy is of the essence until the desired results have been achieved. The Internal Revenue Service holds a taxpayer's return secret by Congressional statute, for the protection of the taxpayer and, by extension, for the safety of the tax system itself. Publication of the Pentagon Papers exposed to hostile scrutiny the methodology of our codes. This section, moreover, in its proper opposition to prepublication restraint, touches with butterfly wings Mr. Justice Stewart's well-argued judgment that once publication has been effected, the publisher should be subject to the penalties imposed by the statutes governing classification. That documents are sometimes foolishly classified does not compromise this position. Without freedom of the press, we cannot have a viable society, but this does not release the press from acting responsibly and in good faith.

Mr. Rook comments:

In a number of instances the report cites examples and assumes facts, while they may or may not be true, which for me as a lawyer have not been satisfactorily established. Therefore questions arise as to some of the conclusions drawn from them.

BACKGROUND PAPER
by Fred P. Graham

Author's Preface

From colonial times to the present, a free press has been recognized—and officially acknowledged in the First Amendment —as a key protector of the rights of American citizens. From John Zenger to John Mitchell legal battles have been fought to safeguard the public's right to know. A corollary to that guarantee, probably more implied than stated, because it was rarely challenged, was the newsman's right to gather news and report, and the assumption that in doing his job he would be secure from government interference or intimidation.

Yet relations between government and press have always and inherently been of an adversary nature. As one commentator has noted, "if anything is clear about press-government relationships throughout our history, it is this: in theory, America's leaders have wanted a free and independent press as a check upon government; in practice, they wanted no such thing." Indeed, it was our first President who spoke testily about "infamous papers calculated to disturb the peace of the community."

While it is true that the press was free, it is also true that it was not always responsible. In its early years, in fact, the press was generally flagrantly partisan. From the time that Thomas

Jefferson somewhat covertly employed Philip Freneau to put out what was essentially an opposition paper—and even before that —the press was in many respects a vehicle of publisher rather than public opinion. It was not until the great press combines, such as the Associated Press, came into being that reporting on a national scale began to strive for objectivity. With the advent of press associations and large urban newspapers, the position of the press shifted; it became more responsible, and the reporter came into his own. His function became more and more investigative— and the number of his antagonists mounted. Although he was sought out for the publicity he could give to both policies and politicians, he was also condemned if his reporting did not please his sources or the subjects of his stories. Yet his role was accorded much of the protection that surrounds the lawyer-client, doctor-patient, cleric-penitent relationships. The state of Michigan even now specifies all four in its statute declaring their communications privileged and confidential.

As the mass media grew more massive and reporting in consequence developed national impact, the status of the newsman became more prominent and more sensitive. So it was inevitable that his presumed immunities would come under challenge. This was never more certain than in the age of confrontation which is now upon us; when the dissidence engendered by the Vietnam war, the emergence of a new "counter-culture" generation and the new consciousness of minority groups find abrasive expression in radical militancy, drugs and social shock of one sort or another.

It is no wonder that society at large would see reason to attempt to control or even suppress the manifestations of this dissidence, that it would call up a more conservative national administration to do the job, and that the press, in consequence, would find itself under pressure to act as witness as well as reporter. The news media soon discovered they had to look to the law for protection: the press could not be free if it were compelled to join hands with government law enforcers. In order to maintain its status as the Fourth Estate and carry out its constitutional duty to inform the public, it had to guard against being used by government as either witness or publicist. And it had to guard against having its freedom compromised by infringements on its confidentiality or questioning of its reportorial impartiality.

It was to this area of conflict between government and press that the Task Force applied itself. Each member had extensive knowledge of some aspect of the problem. Each could contribute his share of expertise, and then the Task Force, as a group, assembled the pieces.

I am deeply indebted to the members of the Task Force for the information and insights they furnished as I developed my thoughts for this background paper. However, they are in no way responsible for the views expressed in the paper. It is my work alone. In doing it I was fortunate to have the research aid of two men with training in both journalism and law: Michael Gross, a former journalism student at the University of Missouri who received his law degree from the University of Michigan; and Richard E. Cohen, a former publisher of the Brown University *Daily Herald* who is now studying law at Georgetown University. I also wish to thank Matthew H. Fox of the Twentieth Century Fund for his assistance and cooperation.

Fred Graham
March 1972

Rights of Newsmen

"Scarcely any political question arises in the United States that is not resolved, sooner or later, into a judicial question." The validity of that famous observation by Alexis de Tocqueville has rarely been better illustrated than by the events that have followed the issuance over the past two years of a series of subpoenas at the request of the Justice Department and local prosecutors, demanding confidential information from the press. The appeals involving subpoenaed newsmen are awaiting decisions by the Supreme Court. Its decisions in these cases are expected to establish important principles regarding the government's power to compel the press to furnish information for the prosecution, particularly in politically charged trials.

But those decisions, as significant as they are expected to be, will touch only one facet of a many-sided issue of governmental power and press freedom that has developed in the past two years. That issue has grown, for the most part, out of the political ferment over racial disturbances, campus unrest and militant opposition to the Vietnam war.

"Group protests, vocal dissent, and the publicity given to them apparently have surpassed the public's level of tolerance."

This conclusion by the authors of a CBS News poll on citizens' attitudes toward the Bill of Rights says much about the reasons for the sudden pressures in the 1970s against traditional concepts of press freedom. According to the poll, three-fourths of the public would bar militant groups from demonstrating against the government. More than one-half of the people interviewed felt that the news media should not be permitted to report stories that the government considers injurious to the national interest. At about the same time, Dr. George Gallup was finding that the public viewed campus violence as the second most troublesome national problem, ranking it just after the Vietnam war.

Against this background—the rising national distaste for radicals and dissent, and the subtle public distrust of that portion of the press that seemed not to be "on the team" with the government against radicalism—Vice President Spiro Agnew began to lash out against the press on behalf of what was called "the silent majority." As the apparent spokesman for the Nixon Administration, the Vice President became a frequent critic of the news media.

The response of the media was sometimes self-righteous, sometimes self-conscious, often derisive as press, radio and TV found themselves on relatively unfamiliar defensive ground. Some media representatives saw justice in various charges made against them, but more feared that the attacks by the Vice President and others presaged an attempt to intimidate the press. This feeling was intensified by a series of events that persuaded many journalists that, as the nation moved to deal with radical elements in society, the news media were in danger of being caught in the middle:

— Government prosecutors, intent on proving that militant groups were seeking to overthrow the government or to assassinate the President, subpoenaed the notes, tapes and files of a number of journalists and publications.

— The Senate Permanent Subcommittee on Investigations subpoenaed the records of a California underground publication to obtain the identity of the pseudonymous author of a number of bitterly anti-police articles.

— Attorney General John N. Mitchell issued guidelines to his prosecutors designed to limit press subpoenas. Two weeks later the editor of an underground newspaper in Madison, Wisconsin, was subpoenaed in connection with the bombing of the chemistry building at the University of Wisconsin.

— President Nixon called news executives from across the country to a news briefing on the Vietnam war—and pointedly omitted major newspapers that had opposed his war policies.

— A number of federal and local intelligence agents were discovered posing as newsmen to collect information about militants, and in a series of incidents legitimate newsmen were assaulted or excluded from meetings by militants.

Similar incidents also took place on the local level, as law enforcement officials moved against black militants and student radicals. But the basic theme persisted; a major national ground swell seemed to be rising against radical militants of the left, and freedom of the press appeared to be in the way. Even before the Justice Department sought to suppress publication of the Pentagon Papers and a committee of Congress undertook to investigate the Columbia Broadcasting System's editing of its television documentary, "The Selling of the Pentagon," four prime points of friction between the government and the press had emerged: press subpoenas, police posing as newsmen, the underground press and the question of the right of access to the news.

Press Subpoenas

"The Department of Justice does not consider the press 'an investigative arm of the Government,'" Attorney General John Mitchell said in August of 1970. Nevertheless, federal and state authorities, before he spoke and since, have been subpoenaing newsmen and their records in connection with grand jury investigations and other criminal proceedings.

"Newsmen recognize that they have an obligation, like any citizen's, to serve justice," *Time* magazine stated. Nevertheless, reporters, publishers and representatives of other news media have continued vigorously to fight subpoenas.

The issuance of subpoenas to newsmen was by no means an invention of the Nixon Administration. Challenges to press subpoenas have been cropping up in American courts periodically for the past three-quarters of a century. But the incidence of such subpoenas has mushroomed since 1969 and spread to state and local law enforcement agencies. The established practice of negotiating and compromising with reporters about just what information would be sought in subpoenas, prior to their issuance, seemed to have been abandoned.

If a random group of lawyers had been asked two years ago what the legal rights of newsmen were to refuse to testify under subpoena in order to preserve the confidence of their sources, probably nine out of ten would have replied "none." For until recently little thought had been given to the legal protections that might be necessary to prevent governmental power from infringing on press freedom. Confrontations between law enforcement agencies and the press had traditionally occurred on a local level, where the press usually had the prestige or the muscle to work things out without going to court. So there was little law on the subject. Only a few reported cases and a handful of statutes existed; for the most part these treated the matter as if all that was involved was the reporter's right to withhold the names of his sources.

That situation changed about a decade ago when the federal government became involved in criminal law enforcement in a major way. Government was powerful enough to think nothing of displeasing even the largest newspaper or network by subpoenaing its files. Even so, few subpoenas were issued until 1969, when the Justice Department, investigating members of several radical groups and needing information about them, issued a series of subpoenas demanding notes, tapes, film, photographs, financial records and personal testimony from representatives of newspapers, news magazines and the broadcast media.

For example, within a one-week period early in 1970:

— Federal authorities subpoenaed the tapes and "out-takes" (film shot but not incorporated into the final product) of a Columbia Broadcasting System (CBS) news program dealing with the Black Panther party. The material was sought for use in a Justice Department case against David Hilliard, a national officer of the party. The next day a second subpoena was issued, demanding a complete record of all correspondence, memoranda, notes and telephone calls made by CBS producers in connection with the Black Panther program. The second subpoena covered an 18-month period beginning in mid-1968.

— Federal authorities subpoenaed the unedited files and unused pictures of *Time, Life* and *Newsweek* magazines dealing with the Weatherman faction of Students for a Democratic Society. The material was sought for a grand jury investigation of disturbances in Chicago during the fall of 1968.

— Earl Caldwell, a *New York Times* reporter covering the Black Panther party in the San Francisco Bay area, received a federal subpoena demanding his presence before a federal grand jury, with notes and tape recordings of his interviews with party officers and spokesmen during the preceding year. The grand jury was investigating possible violations of the laws against threatening the President and against advocating the violent overthrow of the government.

Earl Caldwell's refusal to comply with the subpoena,[1] and the public controversy that arose over it and other subpoenas that had recently been served, seemed to trigger a series of disputes over press subpoenas.

In succeeding months litigation took place over police efforts to subpoena photographs of campus disturbances from *The St. Louis Post-Dispatch* and the student newspaper at the University of Maryland; over press subpoenas sought by defendants in a riot prosecution of "Weatherman" radicals in Chicago; over the Justice Department's attempt to force a reporter for *The Providence Journal-Bulletin* to disclose confidential information about the harboring of the antiwar priest, Daniel Berrigan; over state and federal efforts to compel the editor of the Madison, Wisconsin, *Kaleidoscope* to testify about persons who had placed a notice in his paper claiming credit for a campus bombing; and over the efforts of the Senate Permanent Subcommittee on Investigations to force the editor of a West Coast publication, *Black Politics,* to disclose the name of a pseudonymous author of articles on incendiary devices. The press-subpoena issue became so heated that it produced its own legal side effects: In Palo Alto, California, police officers avoided the subpoena problem by using a search warrant to ransack the office of the Stanford University student newspaper in search of photographs of a student sit-in. The newspaper subsequently sued the police department for violating federal civil rights laws.

Since 1969 press subpoenas have been increasing in both variety and volume. Briefs filed in the United States Supreme Court in the *Caldwell* case revealed that in the first two and a half years of the Nixon Administration, 124 subpoenas were served on the National Broadcasting Company and the Columbia Broadcasting System, plus their wholly owned stations; some were initiated by federal and state prosecutors, others by defense counsel. Over the same period, thirty subpoenas were served on the Chicago newspapers published by Field Enterprises, Inc., two thirds of them on behalf of the government; one *Chicago Sun-Times* reporter, Duane Hall, was subpoenaed to testify in eleven separate proceedings in the space of eighteen months.

Finally, two cases, as well as the *Caldwell* case, are now before the Supreme Court:

— Paul M. Branzburg, an investigative reporter for *The Louisville Courier-Journal*, was subpoenaed by two county grand juries after he wrote articles that described the process by which two young men manufactured hashish and depicted the inner workings of the marijuana trade. He refused to enter the grand jury room to be questioned, claiming that Kentucky statutes and the First Amendment create a newsman's privilege that shields him from compelled testimony. The Supreme Court of Kentucky ruled against him and he appealed to the Supreme Court.[2]

— Paul Pappas, a reporter-cameraman for WTEV-TV in New Bedford, Massachusetts, was allowed by Black Panthers to spend the night in their headquarters during racial disturbances there in 1970. He agreed to report on police methods if there was a raid, but to write nothing if there was not. There was no raid and no report, but he was subpoenaed to give grand jury testimony about the Panthers. He refused and was held in contempt. The Supreme Judicial Court of Massachusetts upheld the subpoena, and he took the case to the Supreme Court.[3]

These incidents illustrate two elements characteristic of recent press subpoena controversies. One is that the government usually resorted to press subpoenas to obtain information about political radicals. The other is that the information being subpoenaed usually went well beyond the identity of a confidential source.

Both elements are important, but the second has had the most direct impact upon the law because it has broadened the area of conflict between government and press. In doing so, it has made obsolete most of the legislation dealing with the relation of government to press that had been passed in prior years.

"Shield" Laws

The most common protection, affording newsmen some measure of immunity from the duty to testify, had been found in state "shield" laws. Passed for the most part during the post-World War II period, such laws have been enacted in eighteen states: Alabama, Alaska, Arizona, Arkansas, California, Illinois, Indiana, Kentucky, Louisiana, Maryland, Michigan, Montana, Nevada, New Jersey, New Mexico, New York, Ohio and Pennsylvania. Most of these laws do no more than give reporters the right not to disclose the identities of confidential sources. The only exceptions are New York and Michigan, whose shield laws protect the reporter from being required to disclose the confidential information obtained as well as the name of the source. The same result has been achieved in Pennsylvania, where the State Supreme Court has interpreted "source" to mean confidential information as well.

The extent to which the political atmosphere in the past two years has complicated the press-subpoena issue is illustrated by these "source" shield laws. They were enacted in the days before the current political ferment by responsible legislative bodies that took what was then an enlightened position in an effort to resolve difficult but rather straightforward conflicts. In most cases, they were inspired by incidents that, in the light of today's situation, seem relatively uncomplicated. Typically, a reporter would write an exposé of gambling, prostitution, official corruption or moonshining and the local district attorney would then be confronted with the necessity to take some action. If he subpoenaed anyone before he called the reporter to a grand jury, it would appear that he knew about the crime all along. So the reporter would be subpoenaed to furnish the name of his informants. A well-publicized squabble would ensue—sometimes terminating in the enactment of a shield law to protect reporters from having to give the names of their sources.

Such laws were, in fact, all the Sigma Delta Chi, the professional journalists fraternity, had asked in its own "Model Confidential Communications Statute." As late as 1963, Sigma Delta Chi's model law included simply the provision that no newsman "shall be required to disclose the sources of any information." This has had such a strong influence upon newsmen's privilege statutes that even the most recent law, passed by Illinois in September 1971, protects only the identities of journalists' sources, and nothing more.

In view of the recent demands for information that have been thrust upon the news media, such laws appear quite inadequate. There are some situations, such as those involving Earl Caldwell and Paul Pappas, in which the names of the sources are well known, but further confidential information is desired by the prosecution. There are others in which government is demanding photographs or television films of riots. That problem is complicated further when the pictures are of peaceful demonstrations that the prosecution claims are overt acts in unlawful conspiracies. Then there are the subpoenas for reporters to testify at trials in which they are asked to tell about acts and speeches they witnessed at protest meetings and where their testimony is sought to lend credence to prosecutors' cases that are otherwise based largely upon the testimony of unsavory informants. Moreover, there is the situation in which a reporter sees an illegal act, such as Paul Branzburg's report of the preparation of hashish, and a judge later holds that the hashish-makers are not protected "sources" but criminals observed in the course of committing a crime.

Consequently, a shield law adequate to the situation facing today's journalists would have to go well beyond any law now on the books in any state. To the public, which might not be aware of the pressures that have produced the calls for greater protection, it might appear that journalists are grossly overstating their case.

There is another element that further complicates the situation. Prior to the advent of the Nixon Administration, the press had on occasion furnished information to the Justice Department. Most often, the information was given quietly, but in a few instances the media and the government engaged in preliminary negotiations that resulted in agreed-upon press subpoenas. These cases covered a range of probes, but the most sensitive were investigations of violence against civil rights advocates in the South and of organized crime.

The fact that the press provided information to Democratic administrations has not been overlooked now that the press is balking at furnishing information to a Republican Justice Department. There is, however, a crucial difference: The information supplied by the press against the Ku Klux Klan and other racist elements was not obtained through confidential relationships. The Klan and the press in the South were at arms-length, to put it mildly; any information known to the press was either second-hand or developed by independent observation.

The present controversy is comparable to the situation that would have existed if, say, the Attorney General of Mississippi had convened a grand jury in the early 1960s to investigate charges that the leaders of the National Association for the Advancement of Colored People or the Student Non-Violent Coordinating Committee were conspiring to incite riots. If newsmen had been subpoenaed to testify about information that civil rights leaders might have furnished about their aims and strategy, there is no doubt that a confrontation over press subpoenas would have come then. The press would have objected that its information was based upon relationships of confidence and trust that would be shattered by disclosure to a prosecutor. Newsmen would probably also have contended that the state had enough evidence to prepare its case without their cooperation and that the state was subpoenaing the press with an eye toward severing the comfortable relationship that existed between the civil rights leaders and the Fourth Estate, thereby reducing the coverage that the movement's activities had been receiving.

At present the press is protesting that the federal government, by seeking to make the newsman a witness before grand jury or court, is interfering with its ability—and duty—to inform the public about black militants, student revolutionaries, traffic in drugs and other social phenomena about which the people are entitled to know. Because confrontation has come on a national scale, the friction between press and government has become more severe. The ground between them has shifted drastically in the last few years, and the law must shift with it in the public interest.

The Duty to Testify

Two basic interests come in conflict when a newsman resists a subpoena. One is the traditional interest of our system of justice in making all relevant facts available for investigations and case decisions. The other is the no less traditional right of the public to a free flow of information through the press. The government, in seeking the newsman's testimony, maintains that compliance with the subpoena is required to serve justice; the resisting journalist responds that his confidential relationships with news sources will be damaged or destroyed and the quantity of information flowing to the public diminished if his compliance with the subpoena is compelled.

The first interest is well established in Anglo-American law. "For more than three centuries now it has been recognized as a fundamental maxim that the public . . . has a right to every man's evidence," wrote John H. Wigmore, the evidentiary scholar.[4] The United States Supreme Court has repeatedly recognized the responsibility of citizens to give testimony and the correlative power of government to compel such testimony. "The giving of testimony and the attendance upon court or grand jury in order to testify are public duties which every person within the jurisdiction of the government is bound to perform upon being properly summoned,"[5] the Court has stated. The principle has been extended to allow testimonial compulsion by legislative committees.

The duty to bear witness is not, however, absolute. Mitigation of the duty may be called for in one of two circumstances, either of which might embrace the case of the newsman seeking to protect confidential sources: (1) where to compel testimony would infringe rights guaranteed under the Constitution, courts may recognize a *constitutional right* not to testify; and (2) where compulsion of an individual's testimony might have a deleterious effect upon a socially necessary relationship, courts or legislatures may be moved by policy considerations to create an *evidentiary privilege* not to testify.

Constitutional Right

The constitutional claim to confidentiality advanced by reporters begins with the proposition that the First Amendment has as its fundamental purpose the enlightenment of the public. Reviewing the origins of the concept of the First Amendment, the Supreme Court once concluded, "In the ultimate, an informed and enlightened public opinion is the thing at stake."[6] The Court has recognized that a central purpose of the amendment is "to supply the public need for information and education with respect to the significant issues of the times."[7] It has also held that "the State may not, consistently with the spirit of the First Amendment, contract the spectrum of available knowledge."[8]

The Supreme Court has recognized several corollaries of the rule that the public must be enlightened. Basically the Court has affirmed that the public's right to receive information must be preserved. To facilitate the public's right to receive information, it follows that the press has a right to disseminate information. The term "press" has been interpreted to mean not only newspapers but also broadcasting and telecasting operations as well as individuals distributing information regarding matters of public interest.

If the press has a right under the First Amendment to disseminate information, it must have a right under the amendment to obtain information. But the newsman's argument encounters its first obstacle on this score because the Supreme Court has never clearly recognized a newsman's right to gather news. In a case decided in 1935 a Federal Court of Appeals recognized a right to gather news but the Supreme Court reversed the decision on appeal—although on grounds other than the First Amendment issue.[9] However, in a series of lower court decisions—particularly those that have been made in the past two years—the courts have assumed that the right to gather news is guaranteed by the First Amendment, and few lawyers expect the Supreme Court to hold otherwise when it confronts the question in the *Caldwell, Branzburg* and *Pappas* cases.

The next step in establishing the newsman's claim is more difficult: to demonstrate that the protection of confidential relationships is essential to news-gathering. The court of appeals in the *Caldwell* case was satisfied that this claim was valid on the basis of affidavits filed by Caldwell and other newsmen, all of whom attested to the importance of confidential information in journalism and all of whom predicted dire effects on news reporting if press subpoenas were allowed to continue unchecked. As the court stated, "The fact that the subpoenas would have a 'chilling effect' on First Amendment freedoms was impressively asserted in affidavits of newsmen of recognized stature, to a considerable extent based upon recited experience."

The affidavits forecast various harmful effects from unbridled compulsion of newsmen's testimony but most predicted a breakdown of communications between newsmen and radical groups. John Kifner, a *New York Times* reporter, described his difficulty in covering the 1969 national convention of Students for a Democratic Society (SDS). He noted that another *Times* reporter, Anthony Ripley, previously assigned to cover SDS, had testified under subpoena regarding the group before the House Internal Security Committee, and that in consequence the convention adopted a resolution barring all members of the "capitalist press" from attending convention sessions. "The fact that Mr. Ripley had testified about the SDS, even though he did not do so voluntarily, was responsible for most of the hostility toward me," Mr. Kifner stated. "It is clear to me that when reporters covering dissenting forces in society are forced to testify about them, their neutrality is compromised and all confidence in them is lost."

Mr. Ripley, the reporter who had testified about SDS, stated in his affidavit that he would have "extreme difficulty" if he ever was assigned again to cover the radical student left "because I will be *persona non grata* with the very persons from whom I must get my news. This is a crippling stigma to me as a reporter."

J. Anthony Lukas, a former *New York Times* reporter who has specialized in covering dissident groups, pointed out the increasing reluctance of radicals to talk with most reporters. "Suspicion and distrust travel rapidly in the [radical] Movement," Mr. Lukas stated. "Violate one man's confidence and sources start drying up all over the place. . . . Thus, if a reporter is compelled to testify about what a source tells him in an interview, he risks jeopardizing not only that source, but all his other potential sources in the Movement.

"Already there are relatively few reporters who are trusted sufficiently by radicals to report their activities," Mr. Lukas concluded. "If these reporters are discredited one after another, the right of the public to know will be drastically infringed."

Several affidavits filed with the *Caldwell* brief predicted or documented breakdowns in news-generating relationships between reporters and members of the black community. Gilbert E. Noble, a black reporter for the American Broadcasting System (ABC) assigned on occasion to cover the black community, predicted that if he were in a position similar to that of Mr. Caldwell and complied with the government subpoena, "it would be impossible for me to go back to the black community and function as a journalist. Since the black community is fully aware of and sensitive to the actions being taken against the Black Panthers, the credibility in that community of myself or any other black journalist who complied with such a subpoena would be totally destroyed."

In another affidavit, ABC reporter Timothy C. Knight described his experiences after being sent to the San Francisco Bay area early in 1970 to produce a television documentary about the Panthers. Mr. Knight said he previously had produced a news feature on the Panthers and had received their full cooperation. This time, however, the Panthers were concerned about the increasing incidence of press subpoenas. They refused to cooperate with Mr. Knight unless ABC News pledged in writing to fight any subpoena of out-takes. ABC News declined to make the pledge and the project had to be scrapped.

Other journalists described the drying-up of confidential news sources within government which might result or had resulted from widespread issuance of press subpoenas. Marvin Kalb, the CBS News diplomatic correspondent, explained that most of the information for his stories derived from confidential conversations. "If my sources were to learn that their private talks with me could become public, or could be subjected to outside scrutiny by court order, they would stop talking to me and the job of diplomatic reporting could not be done," Mr. Kalb stated.

Dan Rather, CBS News White House correspondent, referred in his affidavit to a long-time friend and confidential news source: "This decent, honest citizen, who cares deeply about his country, has now told me that he fears that pressure from the Government, enforced by the courts, may lead to violations of confidence, and he is therefore unwilling to continue to communicate with me on the basis of trust which existed between us."

Prosecutors make several responses to such allegations. They contend that relatively few reporters depend largely upon information from highly sensitive news sources that are highly suspicious of government. Therefore, they say, even conceding that press subpoenas undercut the flow of news from such sources, so few reporters would be affected that newsmen as a class should not be excused from the public duty to respond when subpoenaed. They also argue that the extreme political movements most sensitive to press subpoenas will continue to talk to the press because they need coverage to nourish the growth of their organizations. Faced with the threat that reporters will be subpoenaed, this argument asserts, these groups may stop discussing their illegal activities with the press, but reporters will still be able to give the public the type of news about their legitimate activities that the First Amendment was designed to protect.

When the Supreme Court considers the *Caldwell*, *Branzburg* and *Pappas* appeals it will have as precedents decisions in other cases involving conflicts between the government's claimed needs and the First Amendment guarantees. In the past the government has been required to demonstrate an overriding need before a claim based on the First Amendment would be turned down. If the Supreme Court concludes that press subpoenas must be restricted in order to preserve the public's right of access to information, the Court's remedy could take several forms.

An Illinois state court, faced with such a decision in 1970, set up a series of tests that must be met before a subpoena can be issued against a newsman. In *Illinois v. Dohrn,* a case involving the radical Weatherman group, the court proposed a three-pronged requirement to be met before a newsman might be compelled to testify: (a) the party seeking the subpoena must have probable cause to believe that the particular news medium sought for subpoena possesses relevant evidence; (b) the party must make a showing that the subpoena is the only means available to acquire that evidence; and (c) the party must demonstrate that the evidence is so important that its nonproduction would lead to a miscarriage of justice.[10]

The two lower federal courts ruling on the *Caldwell* case held that disclosure of a newsman's confidential information might be compelled only in the face of an overriding national need for such information. Neither court, however, formulated a test for determining when the government should be deemed to have met that requirement. "We lack the omniscience to spell out the government's burden," the court of appeals stated, noting that the case was one of first impression. It recommended for reference, however, two proposed formulations of the requirement: that of the Illinois state court in the *Dohrn* case, and another, more promising from the journalist's point of view, originating in Caldwell's brief to the court:

> [T]he Government must show at least: (1) that there are reasonable grounds to believe the journalist has information, (2) specifically relevant to an identified episode that the grand jury has some factual basis for investigating as a possible violation of designated criminal statutes within its jurisdiction, and (3) that the Government has no alternative sources of the same or equivalent information whose use would not entail an equal degree of incursion upon First Amendment freedoms. Once this minimal showing has been made, it remains for the courts

to weigh the precise degree of investigative need that thus appears against the demonstrated degree of harm to First Amendment interests involved in compelling the journalist's testimony.

In the *Caldwell, Branzburg* and *Pappas* cases the Supreme Court will confront a sufficiently broad spectrum of subpoena problems to allow it to settle, if it wishes, many of the most nagging press subpoena issues. Both Mr. Caldwell and Mr. Branzburg assert not only that they have a right to withhold confidential information but that the First Amendment also shields them from even having to enter the grand jury room. To enter the secret hearing would damage their relations with their news sources, they claim, because the sources would not know whether they testified or not. The *Branzburg* case also poses the classic question of whether a newsman should have a legal privilege not to disclose the identity of his sources. The *Pappas* case presents a situation in which a newsman's sources are known, but he claims his relationship with them will be threatened if he is forced to betray their confidence.

The Supreme Court could, of course, hold that the First Amendment does not affect press subpoenas; or it could decide the three cases on narrow grounds that will not set precedents. In either case the best way to resolve the problem may be to create a newsman's privilege in the form of a rule of evidence.

Evidentiary Privilege

In order to protect confidential relationships, the courts have been willing in a few special situations to create privileges in the form of judge-made rules of evidence not based upon the Constitution. The most familiar example of such a judicially created privilege is the well-recognized one governing communications between lawyer and client. In order to ensure free consultation between attorneys and their clients, the law has for centuries held that lawyers may refuse to testify about communications with their clients. To a lesser extent, courts have recognized doctor-patient and priest-penitent privileges. There is considerable resistance to extending such privileges because they reduce access to evidence in the courts. For that reason, courts have always rejected the idea of recognizing an evidentiary rule of privilege for newsmen. If the Supreme Court does not resolve the situation, it is probable that there will be a movement to create the privilege by legislative action.

Legislating Privilege: "Shield" Laws. Several bills seeking to establish a federal privilege for newsmen have been introduced into the United States Congress. None has been enacted. There is little doubt that Congress, if so inclined, has the power to create such a privilege. The Supreme Court has held that Article III, Section I, of the Constitution, which gives Congress the right to establish a court system, also implies the authority "to prescribe and regulate the modes of proceeding in [federal] courts."

Eighteen state legislatures have enacted "shield" laws giving newsmen some measure of immunity from the duty to bear witness.* One of the most recent statutes, and for newsmen the most promising, was enacted in 1970 in New York. It provides that:

"[No] professional journalist employed or otherwise associated with any newspaper, magazine, news agency, press association, wire service, radio or television transmission station or network, shall be adjudged in contempt by any court, the legislature or other body having contempt powers, for refusing or failing to disclose any news or the source of any such news coming into his possession in the course of gathering or obtaining news for publication or to be published in a newspaper, magazine, or for broadcast by a radio or television transmission station or network, by which he is professionally employed or otherwise associated in a news-gathering capacity."

The New York shield statute is noteworthy in several respects:

(1) Its definitions of operative words such as "newspaper," "magazine," "news agency," "journalist," and "news" are liberal. Definitions play a critical role in the formulation of a testimonial privilege for journalists.

(2) The statute protects not only the identity of news sources but also the substance of confidential information. The latter is

*The state "shield" laws are reproduced in the appendix.

a vital provision, one lacking in almost all other shield statutes.

(3) The information in question need not actually have been published but merely acquired in the course of news-gathering in order to qualify for the statute's protection. Thus a television newsman presumably could refuse, with immunity from a contempt citation, to comply with a governmental subpoena of his out-takes (film taken but not used in any broadcast).

(4) A shortcoming in the statute from the newsman's point of view may be its failure to protect journalists against having to appear before governmental bodies which might meet secretly, e.g., grand juries and legislative committees; the statute holds merely that a newsman cannot be held in contempt for failing or refusing to reveal confidential information sought by such bodies.

(5) The privilege conferred appears to be virtually unqualified. (Most shield statutes allow the testimony of journalists to be compelled, for example, in the interests of justice or an overriding governmental need.)

Qualifying the Privilege

Whether the newsman's privilege comes into being by judicial ruling or legislative statute, delicate decisions will have to be made on the extent to which it will be qualified, if at all. A privilege against bearing witness provides opportunities for critical evidence to be withheld and justice denied. Yet qualifying the privilege may render it meaningless. The question of qualifications is more than a technical issue.

Definitions are a fundamental problem. The court of appeals in the *Caldwell* case made no attempt at definition but did indicate that Mr. Caldwell's unique relationship of trust with the Black Panther Party, and the unique sensitivity of party members, were primary considerations in its decision.

Most of the state legislatures have at least made efforts to define the class to which the newsman's privilege is to be accorded. The definitions generally consist of two elements: (1) media to be embraced by the privilege and (2) persons within the included media.

Media. Every statute confers the privilege upon newspapers. A few states have set forth criteria for qualifying as a newspaper within the meaning of the statute. The criteria provided by Indiana and New York represent opposite ends of the spectrum. Indiana, which seems to be the most restrictive in defining "newspaper," requires that the publication be issued at intervals of no more than one week, that it be published in the same city or county for at least five consecutive years, and that it have a paid circulation of at least two percent of the population of the county in which it is published. The New York statute is satisfied if a newspaper "is printed and distributed ordinarily not less frequently than once a week, and has done so for at least one year, and . . . contains . . . matter regarded as of current interest, has a paid circulation and has been entered at the United States post office as second class matter."

The definition of the term "newspaper" in a shield statute ought not to exclude the so-called underground press. The Indiana statute, with its requirement of five years continuous circulation and a minimum paid circulation, obviously excludes most underground papers. (It also might be unconstitutional—by denying underground newspapers equal protection of the laws.) Even the New York law, with its requirement of a one-year life and a second-class mailing status, rules out many underground publications. The term "newspaper" has, of course, a common-sense meaning (which probably applies to most underground newspapers), so that even without a formal definition it still can be understood.

Most of the statutes apply to television stations, but less than half apply specifically to radio stations. About half the statutes include press associations; slightly less than half encompass periodicals other than newspapers. The logic of these distinctions, tantamount to discrimination, is elusive.

The purpose of the privilege should be to ensure a free flow of information to the public. All mass media, by definition, are engaged in disseminating information to the public. Instead of arbitrarily limiting testimonial immunity to certain media, it would appear just and reasonable to extend the privilege to all media engaged in the dissemination of information about matters of public concern.

If some selectivity cannot be avoided, it would probably be desirable to protect first those media that disseminate conventional "news." Newspapers, radio and television newscasting operations would then be protected. But if those media are covered, there is no sound reason for not also protecting news magazines such as *Time* and *Newsweek.* And once they are shielded, it would be difficult to justify the exclusion of other magazines. The most logical cut-off point, if one is required, would seem to be books. A person writing a book or doing research for an academic paper is not engaged in a continuing process of bringing information to the public. If he were required to testify, the impact on his journalistic function would be slight. A test case on this issue is now in the lower courts, where John Sack, the author of a book (also serialized in *Esquire* magazine, a further complication) on Lt. William L. Calley, has refused to comply with a subpoena. Relying upon the First Amendment, Mr. Sack refused to produce his notes and tapes of an interview with Lt. Calley about the massacre at My Lai.

Personnel. The statutes vary in defining the categories of media personnel that qualify for testimonial privilege. Michigan accords immunity simply to "reporters." New York protects only journalists who work for "gain or livelihood"—thus excluding most collegiate reporters and photographers. The typical definition is "any person engaged or employed or connected with" a protected medium. Just as it would be less than fair to pick and choose media to enjoy testimonial immunity, so would it be unfair to discriminate among media personnel: the privilege should be available to all persons engaged in gathering, writing, editing, supervising, publishing, broadcasting, televising, or otherwise disseminating information important to the public.

A special problem can arise in connection with the "personnel" of the underground press. Underground newspapers take an expansive view of "staff." When an edition is being prepared, anyone who wanders into the shop is free to help, sometimes even contributing copy. Some professional underground newsmen admit that if a newsman's privilege were recognized by the law, and a "street person" was picked up on a narcotics charge and subpoenaed to testify as to his supplier, the professional journalist might claim that the subpoenaed individual was an underground press reporter so that he would not have to testify.

Dr. W. Walter Menninger, a psychiatrist and member of the National Commission on the Causes and Prevention of Violence, has proposed that journalists be licensed in the manner of teachers, doctors, or lawyers. Although the suggestion was made in another connection—the role of the mass media in encouraging violent behavior—licensing would provide a clear means of identifying persons who could be granted testimonial immunity because of their status as journalists. Qualifications for licensing would have to be formulated, but broadly they might be the same as those suggested above to qualify persons for testimonial immunity. However, licensing has one serious drawback: it would have to be controlled by either the state or the profession, and would present an unnecessary temptation for government or the established press to suppress or coerce the nonestablished, i.e., underground, press. It is useful to note that professions (e.g., medicine, teaching, barbering) are licensed at present to protect the public against incompetent practitioners. It would be difficult to justify on similar grounds the licensing of journalists in view of the constitutional guarantee of freedom of expression, under which competency is hardly definable. Furthermore, licensing might become too much a matter of schooling, training or association with a particular news organization.

Types of information. As a general proposition, it is debatable that the privilege should be extended to all information of public interest that originally was obtained by a journalist in the course of his work, whether or not in confidence. One type of information which would be subject to testimonial compulsion under the above proposition would be a reporter's knowledge of incidents or events which were also observed by the general public. It has been suggested that in determining whether specific knowledge was gained in confidence—perhaps through an "implied confidence"—or was available generally, the critical question is whether the newsman's source could have denied access to the information in question.

Courts and commentators who have recognized the desirability of allowing journalists to withhold confidential information have acknowledged that further limitations on the types of privileged information are necessary. Associate Professor Vincent A. Blasi of the University of Michigan Law School has criticized both the *Caldwell* decision—which would allow compulsion of a newsman's testimony only after proof of overriding governmental need for such testimony—and the Illinois court decision in the *Dohrn* case—which would allow press subpoenas only to avoid miscarriages of justice—because of the *ad hoc* nature of these qualifications. Mr. Blasi suggests that it should be as clear as possible to both newsman and informant just what data may be passed without fear of subsequently compelled disclosure. He has hypothesized a shield excluding "information pertaining to planned future crimes of violence and the whereabouts of fugitive felons," as well as newsmen's observations of crimes to which they were the only eyewitnesses.

An obvious difficulty with this proposal, from the prosecutor's viewpoint, is the unlikelihood that all desirable exceptions to a newsman's shield will be apparent in advance. From the standpoint of radical activists, who often use the rhetoric of violence and are frequently accused of violent intentions, it might appear that they could rarely confide in a newsman without fear that the privilege would be held not to apply. An alternative is to provide for judicial discretion to compel the testimony of journalists in the interests of either overriding governmental need or justice. Many newsmen feel that this approach would render the privilege almost useless, either because judges would be too quick to waive the shield, or because sources would fear that the shield would be waived and therefore would decline to talk to newsmen.

Some shield laws—such as the broad New York statute—make no provision for waiving the privilege. No apparent miscarriages of justice have resulted. Many newsmen believe that no waiver provision is the best solution—that newsmen will usually volunteer information to prevent an injustice. Should a reporter refuse to testify despite a judge's order, he would probably risk a contempt citation but achieve a legal test of his position.

Proceedings in Which the Privilege May Be Invoked

(1) *Civil lawsuits.* The arguments for allowing confidential information to be withheld apply in civil cases. That recovery may be denied parties to civil suits because their prevalence would infringe First Amendment liberties was demonstrated by the Supreme Court recently in a landmark libel decision.[11] In it, the Court imposed a great burden of proof upon libel plaintiffs who are public figures, because such persons are natural subjects of news reporting and to allow them easy recovery might result in newspaper self-censorship and a reduced flow of information to the public.

It has been suggested that the claim of compelling need for a newsman's testimony in criminal cases does not apply as forcefully in civil cases because civil suits generally lack the social impact of criminal proceedings. The markedly dissimilar burdens of proof imposed upon criminal court prosecutors as compared with most civil litigants implies that more is at stake in criminal than in civil cases: criminal court prosecutors must establish their cases beyond a reasonable doubt, while civil litigants, with the exception of public-figure libel plaintiffs, need only demonstrate that a preponderance of evidence is in their favor. However, from the standpoint of preserving justice for plaintiffs in libel suits, the additional burden of proof that the Supreme Court has imposed upon public figures might be impossible to meet if the press could take refuge behind testimonial immunity.

The problem could arise as follows: Under present law, a public figure can recover damages from the news media for defamation only if he alleges and proves that the defendant published false statements knowingly or recklessly. In defense, a journalist might respond that his information was obtained from a reliable informer, and that although it proved to be false, it was not published recklessly. At this point the plaintiff would normally take the newsman's deposition to learn the identity of the informant and to determine his reliability. If the reporter could invoke a testimonial privilege and refuse to give the informant's name, then the plaintiff would fail to meet the burden of proof and his suit would probably be dismissed.

One proposed solution would lift the newsman's privilege when he or his publication is the defendant. Another would lighten the plaintiff's burden of proof when the newsman's privilege prevents him from proving his case.

(2)   *Criminal trials.* The Sixth Amendment provides that, "In all criminal prosecutions, the accused shall enjoy the right . . . to have compulsory process for obtaining witnesses in his favor." It seems clear that where the defendant in a criminal case seeks to subpoena a newsman to obtain confidential evidence, the accused's rights under the Sixth Amendment should be balanced against the harm threatened to the newsman's and the public's rights under the First Amendment. The *Dohrn* case in Illinois involved such a situation and was resolved in favor of the press. In that case the court found that the evidence sought was not essential to the defense and that press freedom might be harmed if a subpoena were issued and disclosure of confidential information compelled.

Many of the same considerations come into play in criminal trials when newsmen are subpoenaed to testify before grand juries. In addition, there is the occasional complaint by newsmen that prosecutors call them to testify in order to dignify a case that is otherwise based upon questionable witnesses. In the federal government's conspiracy prosecution of Dr. Benjamin Spock and others for interfering with the draft, and the case against the "Chicago Seven" riot-conspiracy defendants, reporters were called to testify about events that they had observed in public.

In most instances the prosecution had evidence of these acts, either through television or radio tapes or the testimony of informers or agents who were at the scene. The reporters felt that they were being compelled to appear to take sides by testifying for the prosecution, even though their testimony was not actually needed. The only reason for calling them, they concluded, was to lend the prestige of their names and their publications to the government's case. Because their testimony was, for the most part, not based upon confidential information, a newsman's privilege would not have affected their situation unless it was coupled with a device imposed by the Illinois court in the *Dohrn* case—namely that no subpoena could be issued against a newsman without a showing that otherwise a miscarriage of justice would result.

(3) *Grand jury proceedings.* There are significant distinctions between cases in which government seeks to compel a newsman's testimony at a trial and cases in which the newsman is sought as witness for a grand jury investigation.

One difference is the trial jury's need, and the grand jury's lack of need, for cumulative evidence. Because criminal defendants must be found guilty beyond a reasonable doubt, it may be proper for government to support its factual assertions with evidence from several sources. The grand jury, which makes its decisions on whether and whom to indict on the basis of probable cause, has no such need for reinforcing evidence. Therefore, a grand jury would be less justified in calling a newsman merely to substantiate testimony already given or to give testimony available from other sources.

Another significant distinction is the secret nature of grand jury proceedings. The appellate court decision in the *Caldwell* case indicates that this secrecy may be used to justify not compelling the newsman's attendance upon the grand jury. On the other hand, secrecy has long been recognized by courts and law enforcement bodies as an essential ingredient of successful grand jury investigations. The investigative function of the grand jury has been recognized as central to the maintenance of law and order in society. And it has been held preferable to have the decision whether to prosecute reside where possible with grand juries—autonomous bodies of private citizens—rather than with government prosecutors. The Supreme Court has recognized that a function of the grand jury is "to stand between the prosecutor and the accused, and to determine whether the charge was founded upon credible testimony or was dictated by malice or personal ill will."[12] Thus one might argue that social policy dictates the retention of grand jury secrecy and that the advantage to society of thorough grand jury investigation overrides the harm done by requiring newsmen to appear before grand juries.

One suggested solution to this problem is to allow newsmen to testify in public. The apparent motivation for secrecy in grand jury proceedings is to coax disclosure from witnesses fearful of reprisal or otherwise recalcitrant. Reporters to whom this motivation does not apply could waive their opportunity to testify in private.

Newsmen summoned by grand juries may raise further objections. The Supreme Court has held that grand juries are not limited in their investigations to specific criminal acts; they may call witnesses to testify without having a particular defendant or crime in mind. Such investigations are sometimes known as "John Doe" cases or "fishing expeditions." The Court has also held that grand juries can pursue all ramifications of a particular subject of inquiry, and may thus make much broader inquiry of witnesses than trial prosecutors, the latter being limited in their inquiries to matters relevant to specific crimes. Finally, grand juries are not bound by other rules of evidence applicable in criminal trials. The vagueness of the grand jury's procedural rules makes it difficult for newsmen's sources to predict at the time of their contact just what information may be passed to newsmen without risk of compulsory disclosure.

(4) *Legislative committee hearings.* The Supreme Court has stated the basic case against the newsman's claim to testimonial privilege in legislative committee hearings: "A legislative body cannot legislate wisely or effectively in the absence of information respecting the conditions which the legislation is intended to affect or change; and where the legislative body does not itself possess the requisite information—which not infrequently is true—recourse must be had to others who do possess it. Experience has taught that mere requests for such information are unavailing, and also that information which is volunteered is not always accurate or complete; so that some means of compulsion are essential to obtain what is needed."[13] The courts have also recognized, however, that the investigative discretion of legislative committees is limited by the First Amendment.

The case for allowing newsmen to withhold confidential information from legislatures is similar to that for concealment from grand juries. Legislative committees, like grand juries, are not bound by evidentiary rules. They may conduct their meetings in secret. The primary distinction between the two types of investigations probably is not significant here: whereas grand jury investigations seek to expedite justice, legislative investigations generally are intended to promote enlightened lawmaking. The two aims are legitimate governmental objectives, but both must be weighed against the First Amendment purpose of keeping the public informed about sensitive public matters.

Police Impersonation of Newsmen

In January of 1970 an incident occurred in Saigon that marked the beginning of a new chapter in the relations between government and press. Four agents of the United States Government were found to have masqueraded for two weeks as members of the press corps, apparently in an attempt to uncover sources used by legitimate newsmen. The four, two Americans and two South Vietnamese, had been issued press passes by U.S. military authorities responsible for the accreditation of journalists in South Vietnam. When the four impostors were unmasked by working newsmen, the incident was treated as an isolated case.

"Somebody goofed," was the Army's reaction, in Vietnam. Journalists shrugged off the incident after a few protests. In Washington, Assistant Secretary of Defense for Public Affairs Daniel Z. Henkin termed the accreditation "inadvertent," and added: "It is the unequivocal policy of the Secretary of Defense, of my office and of the Military Assistance Command, Vietnam, to issue press credentials only to bona fide newsmen." In Vietnam the United States Military Command announced that the persons responsible for issuing press passes to the four government agents had been "admonished," and the incident was considered closed.[14]

However, the case proved to be anything but isolated. Within months it was revealed that Army agents in the United States had been using this form of camouflage at least since 1967. It also became apparent that intelligence units of local police agencies across the United States were increasingly using the same ploy for the same purposes.

It was symbolic that this intelligence-gathering tactic first surfaced in Vietnam. For the militant antiwar movement in the United States proved to be the subject of many of the investigations conducted by agents impersonating newsmen. Most of the other instances involved surveillance of black militants. The tactic appeared to be used almost exclusively to gather information about dissident groups, that is, in "political" as opposed to "criminal" investigations.

Law enforcement agencies tend to lack information about political dissenters, who do not fit the traditional "criminal" mold, while newsmen often have easy access to them. Therefore, masquerading as newsmen seems a useful ploy for the police, but it poses a potentially serious problem for newsmen. In the late 1960s and early 1970s, as dissent and violence rose in the United States, came increasing disclosures of police masquerading as newsmen. Barriers of suspicion began to rise between radical elements and the newsmen who wanted to report on their internal as well as external affairs. Journalists were assaulted by militants and excluded from their meetings. The significance of these dissident groups had long been recognized by the Federal Bureau of Investigation. However, unlike many investigative agencies, the F.B.I. does not normally allow its agents to "go underground" to obtain information. Instead, the Bureau relies heavily upon paid and unpaid informers.

For example, in 1967 the F.B.I. quietly added Louis Salzberg, a photographer for the Spanish-language newspaper *El Tiempo*, to its roster of paid informers. Mr. Salzberg began to frequent radical gatherings in New York City, and by 1969 had become so well integrated into the city's radical community that he left *El Tiempo* and established a private studio to supply photographs to the underground press. Among Salzberg's close acquaintances in the militant underground were several of the "Chicago Seven" conspiracy trial defendants. During that trial they were shocked to see Mr. Salzberg called as a key government witness. On the stand he testified that he was more than the news photographer he had represented himself to be. The F.B.I., he said, had given him $100 per month for information until he left *El Tiempo,* then raised his pay to $600 per month. His principal source of revenue throughout 1969 had been the F.B.I.[15]

A week earlier, in the same conspiracy trial, the government had called Carl Gilman, a television-reporter-cameraman for station KFMB-TV in San Diego. Mr. Gilman also testified that he had been a paid F.B.I. informant since 1967, having received between $7,000 and $8,000 for his services and $2,000 for expenses. His testimony included a report on a speech made by David Dellinger, one of the conspiracy defendants, in San Diego.[16]

Mr. Gilman's experience demonstrates the problems that emerge when journalists become F.B.I. informers. When he was contacted by telephone by this Task Force he asserted that his work for the F.B.I. was totally unrelated to his regular professional work. He insisted that he was able to separate his professional and undercover activities, and flatly contradicted press reports that he posed as a newsman. He added that he "very much opposes" military or police officials posing as journalists.

J. Edgar Hoover, Director of the F.B.I., declared in a letter to this Task Force that the F.B.I. has never "actively recruited" journalists as informants.[17] But he conceded that "there is no policy against accepting information from a journalist or any news media representative if it is volunteered, which was the case with Mr. Louis Salzberg and Mr. Carl Gilman." He added that "they were paid for their services and expenses." This explanation apparently means that the F.B.I. will put journalists on the payroll as informants if they initiate the move.

The appearance of Mr. Salzberg and Mr. Gilman as witnesses for the prosecution in the Chicago conspiracy trials created the impression that some people ostensibly functioning as journalists were really gathering information for the police. There is evidence that this episode did much to spread the belief among radicals that inquisitive "reporters" were sometimes policemen in disguise.

However, some government agencies apparently did not have a stated policy like that of the F.B.I. against letting members of their staffs masquerade as newsmen. They recognized that journalism was a handy cover for investigations of radical groups and, instead of using professional journalists as paid informers, began to have their own employees pose as newsmen.

The Army Security Agency appears to have led the way. In its surveillance of what it considered to be radical elements at the 1968 Democratic National Convention in Chicago, the Army, using a fictitious news agency as a cover, painted the name "Midwest Video News" on one of its vans and used it to take pictures of and record interviews with various demonstrators, including Yippie leader Abbie Hoffman. Christopher Pyle, an author and former military intelligence agent, testified before the Senate Judiciary subcommittee on constitutional rights:

> Midwest News had the distinction of being the only television news team at the time of the convention who gained an exclusive interview with Mr. Hoffman, and the talk before the police riot in Chicago. . . . Two agents who were on the team at the time, became very popular throughout the Army Intelligence Command. The Army Intelligence Command used them all around the country. They later came here to Washington and then to Catonsville, Maryland, because they were such a professional team.

Later, during the subcommittee hearings, Robert F. Froehlke, Assistant Secretary of Defense for Administration, acknowledged that Army personnel "were used as photographers under cover of fictitious firms to photograph and record interviews with leaders and members of demonstrations and to film actual demonstrations in Chicago." He also confirmed that the same methods were employed to a lesser degree during the inauguration activities in Washington in January of 1969.

The following exchange at the hearings between Senator Edward M. Kennedy and John O'Brien, a former member of the

113th Military Intelligence Group in Evanston, Illinois, illustrates the manner in which one agent perceived his duty:

Kennedy: *How often would you pose as a newsman when you took pictures of demonstrations?*

O'Brien: *I did it most of the time.*

Kennedy: *Was it acceptable policy at that time (1968)?*

O'Brien: *It is recommended.*

Kennedy: *It is recommended?*

O'Brien: *Yes, it is very easy to pass yourself off as a newsman without utilizing any type of authentic credentials.*

Kennedy: *Is that printed in the training manual by the Army?*

O'Brien: *No—well, that is something you learn in the field, Senator.*

Over the past two years, real journalists have turned up a series of impersonations of journalists that were either admitted or not denied by responsible officials:

Washington—Undercover Agent at Welfare Rights Meeting. On July 10, 1970, Washington reporters covering a news conference held by George A. Wiley, executive director of the National Welfare Rights Organization, noted the presence of an undercover policewoman posing as a news writer. According to *The Washington Post* of July 11, the policewoman, Dixie Gildon, "identified herself to a reporter as Ditty Ayers and said she was a free-lance writer."

While the *Post* did nothing, twenty-eight reporters of *The Washington Star* protested this police policy and pledged to "announce the presence of any police agent we recognize masquerading as a newsman or newswoman," indicating that they would interrupt a news conference to do so, if necessary. They were supported by Senator Alan Cranston of California, who in the Senate on July 14 criticized "this unfortunate practice." As he put it, "this is a serious and growing national problem—one that merits Senate attention."

On July 15 Washington police information officer Paul Fuqua announced a new department policy: "It shall be against the policy of the department for any of its members to represent himself in any way as a member of a news gathering organization."[18]

New York City—Army Spying on Black Militants. Army in-
telligence agents assigned to the 108th Military Intelligence
Group received press credentials from the New York City Police
Department to cover the activities of H. Rap Brown and Stokely
Carmichael in New York during the summer riots of 1967. On
December 31, 1970, Deputy Police Commissioner Wilfred N.
Horne acknowledged that providing credentials to intelligence
agencies was a common practice and that he issued press creden-
tials "to the information officers of all military installations in the
area who requested them on behalf of individuals." However,
Mr. Horne decided to discontinue this policy as of 1971 after a
press credentials committee had discussed the matter with him.[19]

Wichita—Anti-Agnew Demonstration. According to an article
in the January 1971 issue of the *Chicago Journalism Review,*
press credentials were issued to "at least one, and probably four,
local cops" who were taking photographs of individuals spoofing
Vice President Agnew's speechmaking while he was in Wichita
in October of 1970.

Prior to the *Review* article, the Kansas Chapter of Sigma Delta
Chi protested the incident to the White House and received an
apology from Communications Director Herb Klein. Mr. Klein
wrote that he regretted the incident and agreed with the resolution of the national Sigma Delta Chi organization that "indis-
criminate use of press credentials by law enforcement officers or
any others who are not members constitutes interference with
freedom of the press." However, Mr. Klein's letter also criticized
the Kansas chapter: "To blow one incident so out of proportion,
it seems to me, contributes to an erosion of confidence by the
public in the integrity of its elected officials and our democratic
institutions of government."[20]

Chicago—Police Investigation of Black Students. A member
of the Chicago Police Department's "Red Squad" posed as a reporter for *The Chicago Sun-Times* to obtain information from
black high school students who were holding a protest rally to
demand the removal of their white principal. The bogus reporter,
Patrolman John Philbin, was unmasked by the legitimate *Sun-
Times* man at the scene. Joel Havemann, a spokesman for the

police department, said that Patrolman Philbin had been "admonished" and that steps had been taken to see that Chicago policemen did not pose as newsmen in future assignments.[21]

Richmond—Army Surveillance of Civil Rights Spokesmen. The NBC program "First Tuesday" reported on its December 1, 1970, telecast that an Army agent had been issued bogus press credentials representing him as a reporter for *The Richmond Times-Dispatch,* so that he could attend a press conference of the Southern Christian Leadership Conference in Washington. Later, when the *Times-Dispatch* learned of the incident and protested to Secretary of Defense Melvin E. Laird, a Defense Department official sent a letter of regret to the newspaper. The letter said that "upon verifying that this practice had occurred," Army agents were issued instructions "prohibiting the use of press credentials or otherwise representing themselves as newsmen."[22]

Albuquerque—Police Investigation of Campus Demonstration. A city policeman using false press credentials posed as an Associated Press photographer on the University of New Mexico campus during demonstrations protesting the invasion of Cambodia in the spring of 1970. Howard Graves, the AP bureau chief in Albuquerque, complained to the police, who promised that it would not happen again.[23]

Detroit—General Motors Stockholder Meeting. A Detroit investigator posed as a press photographer at a meeting of the General Motors stockholders on May 22, 1970. After the impersonation was discovered, Lt. William McCoy, head of the special investigation squad, explained that the unidentified officer had used the press badge in order to "facilitate movements about the hall during the meeting." Police Commissioner Patrick V. Murphy—now New York City's Police Commissioner—expressed regret about the incident and said that the police department did not allow its officers to pose as newsmen.[24]

Long Island—Police Surveillance of Veterans' Antiwar Rally. Early in 1971 two plainclothsmen posed as newsmen to photograph the audience at a veterans' "Winter Soldier Investigation" at Garden City. After newsmen protested, Nassau County Executive Ralph G. Case issued orders to police not to repeat the impersonation.[25]

Puerto Rico—Police Observing July 4 Parade. Complaints by newsmen covering 1971 Independence Day ceremonies in San Juan that police were posing as reporters to observe the parade led to an admission by the Commonwealth Secretary that his department had been issuing press credentials to police for about eight years. A police official said that plainclothesmen would no longer be given press credentials nor attempt to pass themselves off as newsmen.[26]

Washington—Draft Card-Burning Demonstration. The *Boston Globe* reported that on June 18, 1968, at a draft card-burning event outside the Supreme Court building in Washington a reporter recognized an F.B.I. agent who had interviewed him on an earlier draft card episode as one of a group of "strange faces" among the journalists at the event. The article described the strangers as "men with shiny new hand-held movie cameras and tape recorders who were interviewing and filming the participants along with the familiar faces of the Washington press." The F.B.I. refused to comment other than to say that it was a routine matter for agents to film suspects.[27]

Washington—Congressional Briefing. In the spring of 1971, a man recognized as an F.B.I. agent by a reporter for *The Los Angeles Times* was observed taking notes with reporters at a meeting called by Congressman William R. Anderson of Tennessee to discuss the Berrigan conspiracy prosecution. The man denied he was an F.B.I. agent, insisting that he was a writer, but he ran away when asked by an aide to Representative Anderson to identify himself. The aide followed the man outside the building and saw him enter a car. A check of the license plates later traced the car to the F.B.I.[28]

On other occasions journalists and participants at public meetings have suspected that "reporters" or "photographers" were police agents but could not prove their suspicions. But whether or not these other alleged incidents actually took place, the damage has been done. Many people have come to believe that government agents commonly impersonate newsmen. As a result, the news media have lost access to news sources and newsworthy events involving the politically dissident, and threats of bodily harm have been made against media representatives.

A dramatic illustration of loss of access was the decision of the Students for a Democratic Society (SDS) to bar the "capitalist press" from its 1969 national convention. Representatives of the "revolutionary" press who could be identified by SDS members were permitted to attend. The resolution barring established newsmen from the convention was not passed solely in response to fear of infiltration by police masquerading as journalists, though fear that legitimate journalists, if admitted, subsequently might be subpoenaed as government witnesses clearly played a role in the decision. The radical community had come to identify the press with government, and police impersonation of newsmen clearly contributed to development of this perception. The phenomenon of news sources "drying up," discussed in the section on press subpoenas, has resulted from one form of governmental interference with press freedom, namely, the fear among some groups and individuals that their confidential communications will become available to authorities. Such fear is all the more understandable if sources sensitive to excessive publicity have cause to believe that some of the newsmen reporting on their activities are government agents in disguise.

Joel Havemann, *The Chicago Sun-Times* reporter who unmasked the "Red Squad" agent who posed as a reporter at a black students' demonstration, later put it this way in an article in the *Chicago Journalism Review:*

> Reporters have a hard enough time getting information from groups such as militant black students, who are naturally suspicious of the establishment press. If these groups begin to suspect that every reporter they talk to may be a policeman, our job will become impossible.[29]

The danger that newsmen and photographers may suffer bodily harm as a result of such suspicions is all too real.

In 1969 alone:

— Two California newspaper reporters were hurt in a clash

between students and police near the Berkeley campus of the University of California.

— A *Newsweek* reporter filed charges of attempted assault, harassment, and other law violations against two SDS members in an incident arising out of the spring 1969 disorders at Columbia University.

— *New York Post* photographers were attacked while taking pictures by a delegate to the New Democratic Coalition conference in New York City.

— *Hartford Courant* reporters were forced to abandon their cars and flee from attackers during rioting in Hartford.

— Three newsmen were among those injured during demonstrations at San Francisco State College.

— Student protesters at Roosevelt University in Chicago attacked newsmen, injured two of them, smashed their cameras, and threw a reporter's walkie-talkie out a window.

— Student protesters at City College of New York held a *New York Times* reporter captive for nearly two hours.

Only a perfunctory start has been made so far on efforts to quiet suspicion that impersonations of newsmen by government agents have become pervasive. In several instances, officials faced with a disclosure that one of their subordinates masqueraded as a newsman decried the impersonation and ordered their officers not to repeat the tactic. On March 1, 1971, at the height of the public outcry against the Army's surveillance of civilians, the Defense Department issued Directive 5200.27, which states: "There shall be no covert or otherwise deceptive surveillance of civilian organizations unless specifically authorized by the Secretary of Defense or his designee." This order, despite its "unless" loophole, is interpreted by the Pentagon as prohibiting agents from posing as newsmen. But the prohibition would probably have been more effective in discouraging future abuses by Army agents— and clearly would have done more to restore public confidence in the press—if it had stated plainly that Army agents must not pose as newsmen and had been widely publicized by the Pentagon. Police officials in New York City, Chicago, Detroit, and the District of Columbia have also issued orders condemning impersonations, but again the prohibitions have not been strongly worded.

Moreover, no government has publicly condemned this tactic, except when its agents were caught posing as newsmen. None of the masqueraders are known to have been punished, and it is not clear that any of the new policies against masquerading carry punishment in case of violation.

In short, the recent declarations may not be enough to undo the suspicions that have been created. Radical or dissident groups might well conclude that the expressions of regret by law enforcement officials have more to do with having gotten caught than with condemnation of the practice itself.

To provide some assurance that law enforcement agencies will eschew the stratagems of the past few years in their investigations of militant elements, it has been proposed that sanctions be imposed against any agents who pose as newsmen. At the federal level, Congress or the executive agencies, including the F.B.I., should lay down clear policies against investigative subterfuge involving the media. The F.B.I. and other police agencies would stop employing journalists as informants. It would then be incumbent on the professional journalists' associations to make clear to their members that any newsman who serves as a regular police informer is betraying his public duty as well as his profession.

In certain situations, First Amendment rights and the exigencies of law enforcement may necessarily conflict, but the evidence is that in these masquerading situations they do not. Where police agents have been discovered impersonating newsmen and higher officials have ordered an end to the practice, no one has suggested that law enforcement would suffer. On the other hand, reporters who cover activities of the militant left are aware of the persistent suspicion that "newsmen" may be policemen in disguise.

It is of course recognized that government may need stratagems to determine the intentions of some militant organizations and prevent or anticipate acts of violence such as bombings. The penetration of such groups by undercover agents is nothing new; but the use of newsmen as agents is relatively new—and hazardous. By making journalists suspect, the practice threatens to cut off the flow of information needed to enable the public to make sensible judgments about dissident groups. Conversely, a free press that can be trusted to report on dissident groups fairly may well defuse extreme militancy. The press is a safety valve for dissent that protects both the public interest and the right of legitimate social criticism.

The Underground Press

One of the offshoots of the "flower children" or "hippie" sub-culture that bloomed in the mid-sixties was the so-called underground press. This somewhat romantic label reflected the anti-establishment views of a generation questioning the mores, manners and values of the "straight" society which surrounded it and finding expression in the use of drugs, a "liberated" sex outlook and an unconventional approach to various other aspects of life, from politics to dress. It had its beginnings principally in the centers where hippies congregated, such as Haight-Ashbury in San Francisco and college campuses during the period of the student revolutionary movement.

The underground press has, in a sense, been hoist on its own misnomer, for it could scarcely be called covert. One would be hard put, because of its social context, to put it in a class with the pamphleteering of Samuel Adams and his cohorts; nor is it "underground" in the way that the *samizdat* press of the Soviet Union is. Yet it retains a certain outlaw flavor.

One commentator has described the underground press as "a wildly unpredictable happening: constantly changing and mercurially fluid, it reflects and comments on an era faster moving than any other in history."[30] Another has observed its characteristically radical tone: "Street corner and movement papers, if they are not for revolution, share an abiding bitterness about the State of the Union."[31]

Those who are part of the underground press seem at a loss to define it exactly. When pressed, they fall back to a position similar to Supreme Court Justice Potter Stewart's definition of hard-core pornography: "I know it when I see it." An underground publication, they say, is immediately recognizable as such, by empathy if nothing else. Nevertheless, with its psychedelic art, tabloid size, enthusiasm for some drugs (marijuana and LSD are mainstays of the good life; heroin and amphetamines are poison), four-letter appreciation of sex, and political orientation toward the extreme left, the so-called underground press is clearly anti-establishment. It is the voice of radical dissent in America today.

Numbers are uncertain and fluctuating, but it is believed that there are 300 to 350 underground newspapers that appear regularly across the country, plus about 200 publications that appear sporadically or in mimeographed form. They claim a combined circulation of almost one million readers, and while these readers are usually not the movers and shakers of the communities where the papers are published, the underground press claims to be influential in terms of stirring its readers to action in a way that the established press could not and would not be.

After the "Chicago Seven" defendants were convicted of inciting to riot and contempt of court in the trial that grew out of the disorders at the 1968 Democratic National Convention, only the underground press called for protest demonstrations, which did, in fact, erupt in cities across the country.

Still, in terms of conventional political power, to say that the underground press has little clout is a vast understatement. Underground publications are almost always out of favor with local governments and in bad odor with other influential circles in the communities where they are published. They have a greater proclivity for antagonizing officialdom than the established press, unaccompanied by prestige or self-protective power.

This, of course, is not a new phenomenon on the American

scene. Howard B. Woods, a member of the Task Force, recalls the difficulties faced by the early Negro press some forty years ago. The twenties and thirties, when lynching was in vogue in the South, was also:

> . . . the period of the great national Negro newspapers, notably *The Chicago Defender,* published by Robert S. Abbott, and *The Pittsburgh Courier,* published by Robert L. Vann. There are documented stories published by these two journals that tell of the refusal of small-town Southern postmasters to deliver *Couriers* or *Defenders* to agents in Southern communities. In addition to this, postmasters . . . actually burned bundles of *Couriers* and *Defenders* in the yards of stores serving as post offices. As a device against this, Abbot and Vann utilized the black pullman porter and dining car waiters to serve as carriers. . . . Even then, Southern sheriffs harassed and intimidated agents handling these two newspapers. . . .
>
> Following the riot at Tuskegee Air Force Base in Alabama, the War Department refused to give any information to black newspapers. In addition, the then Attorney General Robert H. Jackson (appointed by [Franklin D. Roosevelt] threatened to close down the black newspaper in Little Rock, Arkansas. John Sengstacke (at present editor and publisher of the *Chicago Daily Defender*) had just organized the Negro Newspaper Publishers Association (NNPA). In his capacity as president, Sengstacke called on the Attorney General and was told that not only was the government going to shut down the Little Rock paper, but also 'a number of others.' With the full weight of the association [behind him], Sengstacke called on Secretary of War Stimson and Secretary of the Navy Knox and created a new respect for the black press. . . . Out of these confrontations, the first black White House correspondent was accredited. He was Harry McAlpin who worked for the *Defender*.[32]

The so-called underground press of today faces difficulties similar to those which confronted the minority press of yesteryear. The domestic tensions created by the changing conditions at home and abroad, which have given rise to a new kind of minority press, have exacerbated the friction between the militants of the "new left" and the government. As the militancy of the underground press has increased in the last few years, so has distaste for it increased in official circles.

An indication of that distaste came in 1970 when Vice President Spiro Agnew paused in a campaign speech to accuse the underground press, along with rock music and various types of books and movies, of luring American youth into a "drug culture." The Vice President declared, "You need a Congress that will see to it that the wave of permissiveness, the wave of pornography, and the wave of moral pollution never become the wave of the future in our country." Less than a month after that the late Senator Thomas J. Dodd of Connecticut introduced a bill to prohibit publication of periodicals that advocate violence against lawmen and overthrow of the government. The Black Panther party newspaper and *The Nola Express,* an underground publication in New Orleans, were cited as examples of periodicals that would be banned. Nor have legislative reactions to the radical press been limited to the United States Congress. In 1970 the Vermont State Senate adopted by a 20-8 vote a resolution calling for the investigation of all underground newspapers in the state.

At the local level, law enforcement officials in some communities began to use their authority against the underground press. They would never have used it against the established press media. They seemed to assume that underground publications forfeited some degree of their protection under the First Amendment when they violated public standards of taste or morality or commented about the police. As a result, a double standard of treatment of the underground and the established press has developed—a double standard that implies unequal treatment under the law.

In August of 1969 the *Los Angeles Free Press* published an official list of undercover California narcotics agents, complete with their ranks, home addresses and telephone numbers. The list had apparently been given to the *Free Press* by a clerk at the state attorney's office. The *Free Press* published the list under the headline "There Should Be No Secret Police." The article acknowledged "the need for police officers," but said that police anonymity encouraged abuses, and cited recent firings of narcotics agents for faking evidence.

At that time California had no law making publication of such a list a crime. The State Legislature passed one shortly thereafter. So the *Free Press,* its publisher, Arthur G. Kynkin, and a reporter, Gerald R. Applebaum, were charged with receiving stolen goods—an offense usually applied to professional "fences" of stolen valuables. A jury returned a verdict of guilty. Mr. Kynkin was fined $1,000 and placed on probation for three years; Mr. Applebaum was fined $500 and put on five years' probation; and the Free Press Corporation was given a suspended $500 fine.

All three have appealed, asserting that the conviction sets a precedent that could be used to stifle the reporting of news since so much of the information published by journalists is based upon documents that are "leaked" without the consent of the "owners" of the documents. The appeals point out that in a similar case in 1969, when Senator Dodd took columnist Drew Pearson to court because Mr. Pearson had knowingly received and published documents pilfered from the Senator's private files, the United States Court of Appeals for the District of Columbia dismissed the suit. The Court said it would be "too great a strain on human weakness" to hold a person liable in damages for merely listening when offered such data.

In a later incident even more analogous to the *Free Press* case, copies of documents stolen in March 1971 from the Federal Bureau of Investigation's field office in Media, Pennsylvania, were sent anonymously to several newspapers by a group calling itself the "Citizens' Commission to Investigate the F.B.I." Information from the documents was published by *The Washington Post, The New York Times* and other daily newspapers. No officials suggested publicly that newspapers might be liable for prosecution.

In October of 1968, police in Dallas, Texas, armed with a search warrant to ferret out "pornographic materials" raided the office of the underground paper *Dallas Notes.* Using two flat-bed trucks, the officers carried away over two tons of material—including back issues of the paper, typewriters and office files. The *Dallas Notes* editor, Bret Stein, was charged with "possession of pornography." The charges were thrown out by a three-judge federal district court, on the grounds that there was no evidence that Mr. Stein intended to print any of the material. The two tons of material were returned only after a suit was filed against the police. Finally, when the *Dallas Notes's* court battles seemed won, the United States Supreme Court overturned on a technicality the lower federal court injunction that had barred the Dallas police from prosecuting Mr. Stein further. The High Court held that the trial court must first consider whether the police raids were threatening Mr. Stein with "irreparable injury" before the court may intervene—a matter that may bog the case down for years to come.[33]

The Police Department of Buffalo, New York, drove the Black Panther newspaper from the streets in August of 1970 by announcing that any vendors of the publication would be arrested. Acting under a 1902 state criminal anarchy statute, the police began their campaign by arresting a street vendor on charges of selling a paper "which advocates the violent overthrow of the existing form of government of the state." "We have been seeking a statute to arrest them under for some time," a police official said. "From now on when [patrolmen] see them selling these papers, they'll arrest them for it." Seven street vendors of the Panther newspaper had been arrested, an American Civil Liberties Union lawyer claimed during the police department's search for an appropriate statute.

Later, two members and a former member of the Buffalo underground newspaper *Cold Steel* were indicted for criminal anarchy and inciting to riot. The riot charge was based on the fact that the cover of one issue featured a photograph of a school building on fire, under the headline: "Back to School." At the time of the arrests, the constitutionality of the rarely used criminal anarchy law was under challenge before the United States Supreme Court. The Court eventually disposed of the appeal without ruling on the constitutionality of the law, and as of this writing the prosecutions are still in progress.

In recent years officials in Los Angeles, Philadelphia, Providence and Richmond have denied press credentials to reporters of local underground newspapers. In Los Angeles, police officials refused in 1967 to issue police passes to the eight reporter-photographers of the *Los Angeles Free Press,* a publication which had a weekly circulation of 85,000. Although the Los Angeles Police Department issues 1,800 press cards and the Sheriff's office 3,000 a year, they refused the *Free Press* on the ground that disaster scenes might become too crowded with journalists, and the *Free Press* did not normally cover "hard-core police beat and fire news." The California courts upheld this action and the United States Supreme Court denied review, with Justices Hugo L. Black, William O. Douglas and William J. Brennan, Jr., dissenting.[34]

In San Diego, in the winter of 1969, *The Street Journal* published a series of muckraking articles—borrowed heavily from an expose that had appeared in *The Wall Street Journal*—about the financial maneuvers of banking interests located in San Diego. Subsequently, the police searched *Street Journal's* offices without a warrant. They arrested more than twenty street vendors for "obstructing the sidewalk" and littering the streets. *The Street Journal's* offices were the object of a series of attacks including .38 caliber bullet holes in the front window, the firebombing of a car, typesetting machinery destroyed and the front door smashed. None of the crimes have been solved. Newsmen involved with the underground press say that such incidents have occurred across the country, and that these represent only the instances that came to the attention of the established press or became matters of court record. Such reports are difficult to evaluate, but the underground press clearly feels that it is being harassed by officials of many communities. *Orpheus,* a bimonthly publication of articles drawn from various underground newspapers, ran a summary of recent incidents involving the authorities and the underground press:

— *Dallas Notes:* Office torn apart twice by cops, in search of "pornography." Cops confiscated four typewriters, cameras, darkroom and graphic equipment, business records, books, posters, a desk, a drafting table, everything that could be ripped loose and carted off. Kept the spoils. Arrested staffers for possession of "pornography."

— *Kaleidoscope* (when in Milwaukee): Editor found guilty

of "obscenity": $2,000 and two-year probation; being appealed. Obscenity law was written especially for paper. Editor's car firebombed and windows shot out. Office firebombed.

— *Great Speckled Bird* (Atlanta): Local Parents' League for Decency starts smear campaign against paper. Leaflet says, ". . . responsible persons are rightly disturbed by the sacrilege, pornography, depravity, immorality and draft dodging. . . . Let's put a stop to this flow of filth before it hurts any MORE children than it already has." City initiates campaign of harassment, threatens grand jury investigation.

— *Xanadu* (St. Louis): Police chief wages war against paper and its predecessor, the *Daily Flash*. One of the editors busted on grass charge by plainclothes cop masquerading as hippie.

— *Kudzu* (Jackson, Miss.): Staff members busted on "obscenity" rap. Fourteen staffers and friends beaten up by deputy sheriffs. Cameras confiscated, paper evicted from office.

— *Open City* (Los Angeles): Editor convicted of obscenity. Gets six months and $1,000 fine. Under appeal. Busted second time, same charge.

— *Every other underground paper in the country:* Salesmen busted, advertising lost, phones tapped, retail shops intimidated, staff members arrested, attacked, or drafted, hassled in every way imaginable.

— The underground press has evolved from the sweetness and light of its early days and is becoming culturally outrageous and politically revolutionary. Its growth has been phenomenal. It has produced anger and fear among those whose interests it opposes.

— As the radical media grow, and as they grow more radical, so do the attempts to repress them.[35]

Another article in *Orpheus* gave the following view of the treatment of the underground press:

> Although these papers have been evicted from their offices and homes, harassed by the police, had their street sellers arrested en masse, had their benefit parties raided, been bombed, burned, beaten, gypped, framed and lost printer after printer, the underground press continues to increase in size and number.[36]

Throughout the underground press account of its grievances against the police runs a thread of revolutionary masochism that makes the complaints difficult to assess. Sometimes the writers seem to see repression because they expect repression. An article in the Chicago *Seed* reeled off a list of "busts and harassment" that included incidents in five cities which, if true, were examples of unjustifiable police bullying. But the article also complained of one raid in which the police turned up illegal weapons, and two other searches that found narcotics. Heavyhanded actions by the police also seem to have followed publication of items that the police could interpret as provocative. In a Maryland suburb of Washington, D.C., for instance, illegal arrests of vendors of the *Quicksilver Times* came after the newspaper printed a cartoon depicting a local judge masturbating.

The loose, communal approach of underground journalists to their own organizational structure also complicates their relationship with the government. They tend to equate their newspapers with the small community of people outside of the "straight" world. The editor of an underground newspaper considers any member of the group a "reporter," a source of news. In Providence, Rhode Island, the two-man staff of an underground paper applied for and received press passes. Then they asked the police chief for twenty-three more press passes and were refused. The refusal was challenged in the federal district court as a violation of the First Amendment. In dismissing the suit, the court noted the newspaper's lack of organization and concluded that a certain degree of discrimination between established papers and "those whose lack of organization is proudly and conspicuously proclaimed" is rational.[37]

This ruling, in a sense, epitomizes the distinction in the public mind between the established and the underground press.

The press pass has always been viewed as a kind of license, carrying with it certain privileges and immunities, and implying that the bearer has met some standard of training that qualifies him as a "legitimate" journalist, able to report the news objectively. Obviously, the doubts and suspicions that the public feels about militant left radicals and the so-called "counter-culture," which openly advocates drugs and other nonconforming practices, are reflected in its attitude toward the organs of these elements in society and their personnel. And although the same public apparently is willing to tolerate established left- or right-wing publications—e.g., *The Worker*—it is not so willing to accept the legitimacy of the un-established, or underground, press.

This same attitude has undoubtedly been shared to some extent by representatives of the established press itself. For it does appear that government has often leaned unduly heavily upon the underground press, and yet the established press has not very readily come to its defense. By not closing ranks with its unorthodox colleagues, the established press may have done the First Amendment a disservice. By permitting public officials to use their authority successfully against publications that incurred their displeasure, the established press has allowed legal precedents to be set that may someday haunt the entire journalistic profession.

Underground newspapers are typically too poor to fend off serious legal attacks. When the Underground Press Syndicate asked its 79-paper membership in 1968 "are you making a profit," only 28 percent said yes. *Open City,* the second largest underground newspaper in Los Angeles, folded in 1970 after its editor had to pay a $10,000 fine for an obscenity conviction. The conviction was later overruled.

More important, perhaps, has been the failure of the established press to throw its editorial weight behind beleaguered underground papers.

There was no editorial outcry, for example, when the Justice Department, shortly after announcing its new guidelines to control press subpoenas, ignored them in subpoenaing Mark Knops, editor of the Madison, Wisconsin, *Kaleidoscope*. In August of

1970, the *Kaleidoscope* ran a statement from a group calling it-self the "New Year's Gang," which took credit for the bombing of the physics building at the University of Wisconsin. The Jus-tice Department quickly dismissed its subpoena and obtained an identical one—this time, its spokesmen said, after going through the procedures required by the guidelines. The same spokesmen refused to say whether the guideline safeguards would be applied routinely in the future to the underground press. Mr. Knops was also subpoenaed by a county grand jury. He refused to testify and spent six months in jail.

When *The Los Angeles Free Press* personnel, in the case cited earlier, were being tried before a jury on charges of receiving stolen goods, the daily press was editorially silent. There was no suggestion that First Amendment issues were at stake. It was not until after the conviction that *The Los Angeles Times* spoke out against an unsavory precedent which it believed had been set.

Such a precedent was written into the lawbooks as a result of the denial of press credentials to the *Free Press* staff. The Cali-fornia Court of Appeals, in upholding the action, reasoned that the reporters had no rights superior to the general public to gain access to the news. It declared:

> Does petitioner's status as the publisher of a weekly paper give petitioner under the First Amendment a right of access to the scenes of crimes and disasters superior to that of the general public? The answer, derived from a multitude of cases, is a clear no.

This was the judgment that the United States Supreme Court let stand, with Justices Black, Douglas and Brennan dissenting.[38]

In all, five cases in which the First Amendment rights of un-derground newspapers were at stake came to the Supreme Court during its 1970–1971 term. In none of them did a member of the established news media or a press organization support the underground publication. Why they did not may have puzzled even members of the Court. As Justice Douglas noted in the *Dallas Notes* case, "If this search and destroy technique [by the police] can be done against this Dallas newspaper, then it can be done to *The New York Times* [or] *The Washington Post.*"

Access to News

Assuring the press access to the news on behalf of the public raises questions that exceed the provisions of the Constitution or the law. (Some of them also far exceed the scope of this paper.) The basic issue is the very fulcrum of the balance between the need for responsible government and the need for a responsible press.

The American democratic system is based on libertarian assumptions and theories holding that the will of the people must be adequately represented and the rights of the people fairly guarded. The foundation of the relationship between government and press is that the free press exists to monitor policy so that the public may judge how well the government is carrying out its mandate and where the law or the electorate must be called in to conserve basic principles and to effect changes. By the simple logic of question and answer the relationship between press and government is necessarily an adversary one on every level of government. For that reason, press-government tension is inherent in our system and the tensions naturally increase as the complexities and dimensions of the role of government increase, thus raising more and more questions about its performance.

Sir Norman Angell once observed:

If people are to be in a position to judge the conduct of their government, to decide whether it is doing well or ill, to decide the merits of public policy at all; if, indeed, they are to preserve the capacity for sound judgment, they must have facts before them not only as the government would have them put, but also as those who disagree with the government may desire to put them.[39]

The United States Supreme Court, in Grosjean v. American Press Co., (1936), put it this way:

The predominant purpose of the grant of immunity here invoked was to preserve an untrammeled press as a vital source of public information. The newspapers, magazines and other journals of the country, it is safe to say, have shed and continue to shed, more light on the public and business affairs of the nation than any other instrumentality of publicity; and since informed public opinion is the most potent of all restraints upon misgovernment, the suppression or abridgment of the publicity afforded by a free press cannot be regarded otherwise than with grave concern.[40]

On the basic premise that a free press must exist to seek out the news of government and to inform the people, it is clear that there are two basic obstacles that lie in the way of the press:

(1) Government has the power to initiate news, to determine what shall be made public, and thus, in effect, the power to manipulate the news; and

(2) Government may have reason, if not a duty, to keep some of its affairs secret, raising the question of who is to judge what should be kept secret and when it is legitimate for the press to breach such secrecy.

Efforts by the press to negotiate these obstacles put reciprocal pressures on press and government which in effect put the First Amendment right continually to the test as the government tries to limit and the press seeks to advance it.

Two incidents involving breaches of government secrecy have recently mushroomed, resulting in an extreme rise in tension between press and government. The first was the affair of the so-called Pentagon Papers, which the Task Force has explored in its report. The second and, at this writing, current, case is the publication by Washington columnist Jack Anderson of the minutes of meetings held by the Special Action Group of the National Security Council on the handling of the India-Pakistan war over Bangladesh.

No legal moves have yet been made in the latter case, as they have in the former, but both are glaring instances of attempts by the press to reveal the inner workings of government in the making of policies which are of great public concern. Just as the subpoena cases test how far a newsman may go in refusing to be used by government lest his function as a journalist be jeopardized, so do these incidents pose the problem of what limits can be placed on press freedom. It is clear, without going into the merits of either case, that these incidents have increased the danger that the balance between the public's right to know and the government's need to conduct its affairs responsibly could be upset if either government or press react at one extreme or another.

Another matter, somewhat less sensitive, has also come to the fore recently. This is the issue of the "backgrounder"—news briefings by government officials that may be reported but without attribution except in the arch terms of "informed sources," "high government officials," "an Administration source" and other such euphemisms. The background briefing again raises the problem that the press may be used by government to manipulate the news to the detriment of public confidence in the media.

"The most controversial use of backgrounders," wrote Bernard Gwertzman in *The New York Times*[41] "has been the attempt by various Administrations to defend or promote their policies in such a way that the news media serve as the mouthpiece for the Government." Another criticism of the backgrounder, Mr. Gwertzman continued, "is that the identity of the person meeting with newsmen usually is widely known to Washington journalists, their editors, Government officials, diplomats and many other interested parties soon after the event, but not to the public."

A. M. Rosenthal, managing editor of *The Times,* in a statement on the issue, said, "The use of information from confidential or unnamed sources is essential to the press. Otherwise, facts vital to an informed public might never become known. . . . But the problem arises when Government officials or politicians call reporters together and in advance lay down conditions of nonattribution. Often the real purpose is simply to float trial balloons or to present an attitude or a policy without taking the responsibility for standing behind them. . . . The result often is concealment of sources not on the basis of real need for confidentiality but to suit the political or diplomatic convenience of the government or political sources."[42]

The issue arose when first *The Washington Post* and then *The New York Times* refused to abide by the traditional ground rules for these briefings and revealed that Henry Kissinger, President Nixon's confidential adviser, was the source of a suggestion that the President might reconsider a planned summit meeting in Moscow, a possibility that was denied once it was published.

The reaction of *The Washington Posts's* executive editor, Benjamin C. Bradlee, was to issue guidelines for his reporters "to get this newspaper once and for all out of the business of distributing the party line of any official of any government without identifying that official and that government."[43]

However, in the matter of backgrounders, the press and the government seem agreed that some kind of ground rules will solve the problem—although Bill Moyers, former press secretary to President Lyndon Johnson, doubts they will be effective.

The problem of access to the news has other aspects which, though less spectacular, are just as important because they go to the heart of the daily task of keeping the public informed.

In a widely quoted speech in the spring of 1971 on "The Necessity for Civility," Chief Justice Warren E. Burger recalled that despite the current tensions that exist between the elements of the legal profession, public officials and the press, things have been worse in the past. In the nineteenth century, he noted, "news media were intensely partisan and vicious and it was not uncommon for political leaders to horsewhip newspaper reporters." Horsewhipping has gone out of style in dealings between officialdom and the press, but the tensions have not; many officeholders are known to yearn to exclude unfriendly journalists from the scene. However, few public officials have moved openly to deny the press access to the news. Whether a sense of fair play, a reluctance to antagonize the press, or a concern for the First Amendment is responsible, most officials do not question the assumption that all newsmen must be given equal access to news events and records.

A high-level departure from the spirit, if not the letter, of this tradition came in June of 1970, when President Nixon invited representatives of forty newspapers and broadcasting networks to a background briefing on American operations in Indochina. No representative from either *The New York Times* or *The Washington Post,* both frequent critics of the war in Vietnam, was invited. The *Times* and *Post* challenged their exclusion from the briefing and were told that the selection of invitees reflected an effort to have a geographical cross-section of the country represented. One other paper from Washington and one from New York had been invited, the *Times* and *Post* were told, and the policy had been to invite no more than one representative from any city. Yet the list of media representatives attending the briefing revealed that two had been invited from both Chicago and Dallas.

More recently, the President held a White House news briefing which was attended by only nine columnists, all of a generally conservative bent. Although the President's news briefings were not public meetings, they were official news events and the suspicion was inescapable that access to them was denied to those who had not reported the news as the President liked to read it.

In November of 1971, the White House denied a press pass on security grounds to Thomas K. Forcade, who is the Washington representative for the Underground Press Syndicate and, incidentally, a member of the Task Force. White House spokesmen would give no details as to why Mr. Forcade was excluded. A Secret Service official explained that "it was simply a case of what's best in the interest of our protective mission."

Mr. Forcade's case is a difficult one because, following the custom of the radical press, he has felt no need to confine himself to the neutrality that traditionally has been the posture of the journalist. He claims to be a member of both the Weatherman faction of the Students for a Democratic Society and the radical White Panther party. Both groups have been involved in violent incidents, but Mr. Forcade insists that he is a "non-violent person" who has never taken part in the planning or execution of a violent act. He has, however, been involved in one widely publicized incident that set him apart from most journalists' standards of decorum, to say the least. In the spring of 1970 he threw a pie in the face of Otto Larsen, a member of the United States Commission on Obscenity and Pornography, during a public hearing of the commission. He later explained that he had been asked to testify and was trying to make the point that the idea of the commission was ludicrous.

Nevertheless, the fact remains that journalists may be denied access to the news because of their associations with radical groups and individuals. This problem, of course, is of particular importance to the underground press. But it is a question that should be resolved.

Chief Justice Burger himself has not escaped criticism for restricting newsmen's access to information. The Chief Justice usually excludes radio and television newsmen when he speaks in public. When questioned about the practice, he said that the bright lights used by television crews distract him and that he fears the portions of his speeches ultimately broadcast would be distorted because they might be recorded out of context. Chief Justice Burger said he thought newspaper coverage of his speeches was more satisfactory because newspapers have more time for editing and some papers are using reporters with some legal knowledge to cover Supreme Court business.

The Chief Justice came under fire from newsmen again after the Supreme Court issued reprints in pamphlet form of his 1970 State of the Judiciary address. The reprints bore the stipulation, "Not to be reprinted without permission." Chief Justice Burger claimed, however, that no one had been denied permission to reprint the speech.

Questions of newsmen's access to news have so rarely been the subject of litigation that the very existence of a general First Amendment right of access remains in question. In its decision denying press credentials to *The Los Angeles Free Press*, the Court of Appeals of California stated—without feeling the need to cite supporting authority—that the First Amendment does not give the press "a right of access to the scenes of crimes and disaster superior to that of the general public."[44]

It seems apparent that, as matters now stand, courts will uphold the right of federal or state officials to bar either all newsmen or all newsmen and the general public from official events, if such action is motivated by a proper governmental purpose. Two courts have rendered such rulings. When a New York judge closed a trial to both press and public in the interest of "good morals," newsmen challenged the order. The State Supreme Court denied their claim, finding that the First Amendment had "never been held to confer upon the press a constitutionally protected right to access to sources of information not available to others." That passage was cited and the decision followed by a Federal Court of Appeals in upholding a lower court order which prohibited picture-taking in and around courtrooms.

However, when access has been granted to some reporters, the courts have uniformly held that it cannot be arbitrarily denied to others.

In 1965, after the Tennessee legislature passed a resolution barring all reporters representing the *Nashville Tennessean* from its sessions, the United State District Court held that the First Amendment had been violated. The resolution, passed to punish the newspaper after one of its reporters had refused to leave a secret Senate committee session, was intended to remain in effect until the newspaper sent a letter to the Senate promising to "abide by" all rules of the Tennessee legislature. Finding that the Senate could more easily have passed a resolution barring all reporters from secret proceedings, the court overturned the legislature's action as unduly restricting freedom of the press.[45]

The state courts of Alabama took the same course in 1970 when local authorities in Anniston denied *Anniston Star* reporters access to city records. The *Star* had recently exposed a misdeed within the city government. The state courts ordered the city to allow reporters reasonable access to public records. Similarly, when the Stafford County, Virginia, Board of Supervisors banned the publisher of a local taxpayers' newsletter and his tape recorder from their meetings, a state court declared that the First Amendment had been violated and ordered the Board to admit the part-time journalist and his recorder to all meetings that were open to the public and the press.

Such court decisions, however, affect only the extraordinary instance in which public officials have openly discriminated against certain journalists. Most newsmen feel that there is a danger that they may lose access to important governmental information not through the public slamming of official doors, but through a gradual process of bureaucratic smothering of pores of information. The fear is that as governmental bureaucracies inevitably grow, burying responsible personnel below an ever-thickening layer of official "spokesmen," the ability of journalists to report intelligently about governmental operations will become increasingly blunted.

As Zechariah Chaffee, Jr., has noted:

In many subjects the complexity of the pertinent facts increases. Equal access to the facts becomes more and more difficult. The power of government over the sources of information tends to grow. Hence the misuse of this power by government becomes a more and more serious danger. . . . On the other hand, a modern government makes great demands for secrecy. Of course, state secrets are nothing new. Military information was always guarded from the enemy, and bureaucrats have often invoked public safety as a protection from criticism. What is significant is the enormous recent expansion of the subjects which officials are seeking to hide from publication until they give the signal.[46]

In 1967 Congress attempted to deal with this problem through enactment of the Freedom of Information Act. It requires the agencies of the executive branch (but not Congress or the courts) to make available to the public and the press certain records and procedures. However, the law has generally been considered a disappointment by the press. In most agencies the procedures have undergone no noticeable change, and officials have been known to react with amused incredulity when, on the strength of the law, newsmen demanded certain data. The law is laced with exceptions that preclude the release of national security information, internal documents, law enforcement material and other types of information. But the primary drawback is that newsmen can enforce their demand for information only by going to court. Few of them wish to spend their time and resources in this way. So until a quicker, less expensive means of enforcing the right to information is devised, the current law will not be an adequate answer to the problem of free access to the news.

Conclusion

The tensions touched off by Vice President Agnew's speeches criticizing the news media and the flurry of press subpoenas in 1969 suggested to many that press freedom can be more fragile than had been supposed. But reported from the perspective of American history, executive strictures on the press are not unique. In this case, they were the inevitable concomitant of the unrest and violence that resulted from the prolonged United States involvement in the Vietnam war, from the black civil rights movement, the emergence of a new "counter-culture" of youth, and the activism of the student revolutionaries that congealed in the radical militancy of the New Left.

The public at large—what came to be called the "silent majority"—dismayed at the eroding image of the United States, had called upon a conservative administration to arrest that erosion, and the administration was quick to respond.

In the ensuing attempts to prosecute the activists and investigate the radicals, the law enforcement agencies called upon the press as witness. The result was litigations as the press fought against becoming an arm of the law. At the same time, the status of the underground press also came into question. Apart from the clash with law enforcement agencies, the press pushed into the area of national security by intensifying its role as public informant and publishing excerpts from classified studies and minutes of meetings concerning foreign policy past and present, thus spotlighting the question of the limits of freedom of the press.

The attacks on the news media and their confrontations with law enforcement agencies did succeed in demonstrating (1) that the press could not count on the blanket guarantee of freedom contained in the First Amendment; (2) that any threat to that basic right had to be met, usually in the courts; and (3) that many aspects of press freedom as well as the powers and prerogatives of government in relation to the press had yet to be clearly defined.

The protections afforded the broadcast media by the First Amendment against governmental action or pressure are ambiguous—especially since government, through the Federal Communications Commission, regulates those media. The television industry in particular, now the most massive of the mass media in terms of the audience reached by its news and special events programs and their national impact, has been alerted to any attempts by government to infringe on its freedom to inform the people. But it has also been made aware of its own responsibility to maintain proper journalistic standards lest its general entertainment role eclipse its reporting function.

The vulnerability of the news media seems to flow largely from uncertainties about the rights and responsibilities of both press and government. In each of the four major problem areas discussed—subpoenas of the press, police or government agents impersonating newsmen, the so-called underground press, and access to the news—friction developed because these rights and responsibilities are uncertain and the question has now reached the Supreme Court. Rules against police impersonation of newsmen have not been laid down. Public officials and the established press have been ambivalent about the journalistic status of the underground press. Access to the news and news sources remain a volatile and amorphous area of press-government relations, especially in regard to how far the press can go in breaching government security in matters that typically involve foreign affairs and defense.

It is important that such frictions do not become corrosive. They probably will not if the rights and responsibilities of press and government are understood, made part of the law codes and quickly adjudicated when necessary. In any conflict between power and freedom, the proper balance can be struck only through a faithful adherence to the rule of law.

Yet it must be recognized that judgments of the law are inherently interpretive. David Grey, professor of communications at Stanford University, has noted that "the inability to 'prove' the law means that law is never really fully settled."[47] The interpretation of the law in an area as sensitive as press-government relations is often a matter of time and place. The movement of events, current ideology, the state of law and order, legal precedents, a judge's personality and beliefs, social conditions, world outlook—all become factors in the application of law to particular circumstances. That is why law is always under challenge and why first principles are so vital. One of the essential first principles that must concern the citizens of a democracy is that the press remain free. It will always be under pressure; the important thing is that it never be suppressed.

Notes to Background Paper

1. United States v. Caldwell, 434 F. 2d 1081 (9th Cir. 1970), *cert. granted*, 402 U.S. 942 (1971).

2. Branzburg v. Hayes, 461 S.W. 2d 345 (Ky. Ct. of App. 1971), *cert. granted*, 402 U.S. 942 (1971).

3. In re Pappas, 266 N.E. 2d 287 (1971), *cert. granted*, 402 U.S. 942 (1971).

4. John H. Wigmore, *Evidence*, section 2192 (McNaughton Rev. 1961).

5. Blair v. United States, 250 U.S. 273, 281 (1919).

6. Grosjean v. American Press Company, Inc., *et al.*, 297 U.S. 233, 247 (1936).

7. Thornhill v. Alabama, 310 U.S. 88, 102 (1940).

8. Griswold v. Connecticut, 381 U.S. 479, 482 (1965).

9. Associated Press v. KVOS, 80 F. 2d 585 (9th Cir. 1935), rev'd 299 U.S. 269 (1936).

10. People v. Dohrn, Crim. No. 69-3808 (Cir. Ct. Cook City Ill., May 20, 1970).

11. *The New York Times* v. Sullivan, 376 U.S. 254 (1964).

12. Hale v. Henkel, 201 U.S. 43, 59 (1906).

13. McGrain v. Daugherty, 273 U.S. 135, 175 (1927).

14. *The New York Times*, January 29, 1970, p. 12; January 30, 1970, p. 7.

15. *The New York Times*, October 24, 1969, p. 28.

16. *Ibid.*

17. Letter from John W. Hushen, Director of Information, Justice Department, to Matthew H. Fox, Twentieth Century Fund, dated June 7, 1971.

18. *The Washington Post*, July 16, 1970, p. A3.

19. *The New York Post*, December 31, 1970, p. 2.

20. Ron Dorfman, "Watching the Watchers," *The Chicago Journalism Review*, January 1971, p. 3. See also Bruce J. Quodes, "The Press-Card Disguise," *The Nation*, November 30, 1970, p. 561.

21. *The Chicago Sun-Times*, March 13, 1971, p. 16.

22. *The Washington Post*, April 23, 1971, p. A13.

23. *The New York Times*, March 29, 1971, p. 21.

24. *The Grand Rapids Press*, May 27, 1970, p. 8; June 12, 1970, p. 12.

25. *The New York Guild Reporter*, February 11, 1971, p. 3.

26. *Editor and Publisher*, June 31, 1971.

27. *The Boston Globe*, June 18, 1968, p. 1.

28. *The Los Angeles Times*, May 20, 1971, p. 5.

29. *The Chicago Journalism Review*, April 1971, p. 13.

30. Robert J. Glessing, *The Underground Press in America*, Indiana University Press, Bloomington (1970), p. 5.

31. Ethel G. Romm, *Open Conspiracy*, K. S. Giniger Co., New York (1970), p. 25.

32. Letter from Howard B. Woods, editor and publisher, *St. Louis Sentinel*, dated November 9, 1971.

33. Dyson v. Stein, 401 U.S. 200 (1971).

34. *The Los Angeles Free Press, Inc.* v. City of Los Angeles, 9 Cal. App. 3d 488, 88 Cal. Rptr. 605 (1970), *cert. denied*, 401 U.S. 982 (1971).

35. *Orpheus*, Volume 2, Number 2, p. 11.

36. *Orpheus*, Volume 1, Number 4, p. 19.

37. Strasser v. Doorly, 6CRL 2425 (DC R.I., February 25, 1970).

38. *The Los Angeles Free Press* v. City of Los Angeles, *op. cit.*

39. Sir Norman Angell, *The Press and the Organization of Society*, London (1922), p. 22. Cited in *The People's Right to Know*, Legal Access to Public Records and Proceedings, by Harold L. Cross, Columbia University Press (1953).

40. Grosjean v. American Press Company, Inc., *et al.*, 297 U.S. 233, 56 S. Ct. 444, 80 L. Ed. 660, 665 (1936), *op. cit.*

41. *The New York Times*, December 17, 1971, p. 26.

42. *Ibid.*

43. *Ibid.*

44. *The Los Angeles Free Press* v. City of Los Angeles, *op. cit.*

45. Kovach v. Maddox, 33 USLW 2461, (M.D. Tenn., February 22, 1965).

46. Zechariah Chaffee, Jr., *Government and Mass Communications*, Volume 1, Chicago (1947), pp. 12, 13. See citation, footnote 38.

47. David L. Grey, *The Supreme Court and the News Media*, Northwestern University Press (1968), p. 25.

Appendices

Appendix 1

State Shield Laws Currently in Effect

ALABAMA—Code title 7, § 370 (1960):

§ 370. *Newspaper, radio and television employees.*—No person engaged in, connected with, or employed on any newspaper (or radio broadcasting station or television station) while engaged in a news gathering capacity shall be compelled to disclose, in any legal proceeding or trial, before any court or before a grand jury of any court, or before the presiding officer of any tribunal or his agent or agents, or before any committee of the legislature, or elsewhere, the sources of any information procured or obtained by him and published in the newspaper (or broadcast by any broadcasting station or televised by any television station) on which he is engaged, connected with, or employed.

ALASKA—Statutes § 09.25.150, 160 (Supp. 1970):

Sec. 09.25.150. *Claiming of privilege by public official or reporter.* Except as provided in §§ 150-220 of this chapter. No public official or reporter may be compelled to disclose the source of information procured or obtained by him while acting in the course of his duties as a public official or reporter.

Sec. 09.25.160. *Challenge of privilege.* (a) When a public official or reporter claims the privilege in a cause being heard before the supreme court or a superior court of this state, a person who has the right to question him in that proceeding, or the court on its own motion, may challenge the claim of privilege. The court shall make or cause to be made whatever inquiry the court thinks necessary to a determination of the issue. The inquiry may be made instanter by way of questions put to the witness claiming the privilege and a decision then rendered, or the court may require the presence of other witnesses or documentary showing or may order a special hearing for the determination of the issue of privilege.

(b) The court may deny the privilege and may order the public official or the reporter to testify, imposing whatever limits upon the testimony and upon the right of cross-examination of the witness as may be in the public interest or in the interest of a fair trial, if it finds the withholding of the testimony would

(1) result in a miscarriage of justice or the denial of a fair trial to those who challenge the privilege; or

(2) be contrary to the public interest.

ARIZONA—Rev. Stat. Ann. § 12-2237 (Supp. 1970):

§ 12-2237. *Reporter and informant:* A person engaged in newspaper, radio, television or reportorial work, or connected with or employed by a newspaper, radio or television station, shall not be compelled to testify or disclose in a legal proceeding or trial or any proceeding whatever, or before any jury, inquisitorial body or commission, or before a committee of the legislature, or elsewhere, the source of information procured or obtained by him for publication in a newspaper or for broadcasting over a radio or television station with which he was associated or by which he is employed. As amended Laws 1960, Ch. 116.

ARKANSAS—Stat. Ann. § 43-917 (1964):

§ 43-917. *Newspaper or radio privilege.* Before any editor, reporter, or other writer for any newspaper or periodical, or radio station, or publisher of any newspaper or periodical or manager or owner of any radio station, shall be required to disclose to any Grand Jury or to any other authority, the source of information used as the basis for any article he may have written, published or broadcast, it must be shown that such article was written, published or broadcast in bad faith, with malice, and not in the interest of the public welfare.

CALIFORNIA—Evid. Code § 1070 (1966):

§ 1070. *Newsman's refusal to disclose news source.* A publisher, editor, reporter, or other person connected with or employed upon a newspaper, or by a press association or wire service, cannot be adjudged in contempt by a court, the Legislature, or any administrative body, for refusing to disclose the source of any information procured for publication and published in a newspaper.

Nor can a radio or television news reporter or other person connected with or employed by a radio or television station be so adjudged in contempt for refusing to disclose the source of any information procured for and used for news or news commentary purposes on radio or television.

§ 1070 (as amended April 16, 1971). A publisher, editor, reporter, or other person connected with or employed upon a newspaper, or by a press association or wire service, or any person who has been so connected or employed, cannot be adjudged in contempt by a court, the Legislature, or any administrative body, for refusing to disclose the source of any information procured while so connected or employed for publication in a newspaper.

Nor can a radio or television news reporter or other person connected with or employed by a radio or television station, or any person who has been so connected or employed, be so adjudged in contempt for refusing to disclose the source of any information procured while so connected or employed for news or news commentary purposes on radio or television.

ILLINOIS—Public Law 71-1623, approved September 23, 1971:

Section. 1. No court may compel any person to disclose the source of any information obtained by a reporter during the course of his employment except as provided in this Act. The privilege conferred by this Act is not available in any libel or slander action in which a reporter or news medium is a party defendant.

Section 2. As used in this Act:

a. "reporter" means any person regularly engaged in the business of collecting, writing or editing news for publication through a news medium; and includes any person who was a reporter at the time the information sought was procured or obtained.

b. "news medium" means any newspaper or other periodical issued at regular intervals and having a paid general circulation; a news service; a radio station; a television station; a community antenna television service; and, any person or corporation engaged in the making of news reels or other motion picture news for public showing.

c. "source" means the person or means from or through which the news or information was obtained.

Section 3. In any case where a person claims the privilege conferred by this Act, the person or party, body or officer, seeking the information so privileged, may apply in writing to the circuit court serving the county where the hearing, action or proceeding in which the information is sought for an order divesting the person named therein of such privilege and ordering him to disclose his source of the information.

Section 4. The application provided in Section 3 of this Act shall allege: the name of the reporter and of the news medium with which he was connected at the time the information sought was obtained; the specific information sought and its relevancy to the proceedings; and, a specific public interest which would be adversely affected if the factual information sought were not disclosed.

Section 5. All proceedings in connection with obtaining an adjudication upon the application not otherwise provided in this Act shall be governed by the Civil Practice Act.

Section 6. In granting or denying divestiture of the privilege provided in this Act the court shall have due regard to the nature of the proceedings, the merits of the claim or defense, the adequacy of the remedy otherwise available, if any, the relevancy of the source, and the possibility of establishing by other means that which it is alleged the source requested will tend to prove.

Section 7. An order granting divestiture of the privilege provided in this Act shall be granted only if the Court, after hearing the parties, shall find:

(a) that the information sought does not concern matters, or details in any proceeding, required to be kept secret under the laws of this State or of the Federal government; and

(b) that all other available sources of information have been exhausted and disclosure of the information sought is essential to the protection of the public interest involved.

If the court enters an order divesting the person of the privilege granted in this Act it shall also order the person to disclose the information it has determined should be disclosed.

Section 8. An order entered under this Act is appealable the same as a comparable order in a civil case under Supreme Court Rules and is subject to being stayed. In case of an appeal the privilege conferred by this Act remains in full force and effect during the pendency of such appeal.

Section 9. A person refusing to testify or otherwise comply with the order to disclose the source of the information as specified in such order, after such order becomes final, may be adjudged in contempt of court and punished accordingly.

INDIANA—Stat. Ann. § 2-1733 (1968):

2-1733. *Newspapers, television and radio stations—Press associations—Employees and representatives—Immunity.*—Any person connected with a weekly, semiweekly, triweekly or daily newspaper that conforms to postal regulations, which shall have been published for five [5] consecutive years in the same city or town and which has a paid circulation of two per cent [2%] of the population of the county in which it is published, or a recognized press association, as a bona fide owner, editorial or reportorial employee, who receives his or her principal income from legitimate gathering, writing, editing and interpretation of news, and any person connected with a commercially licensed radio or television station as owner, official, or as an editorial or reportorial employee who receives his or her principal income from legitimate gathering, writing, editing, interpreting, announcing or broadcasting of news, shall not be compelled to disclose in any legal proceedings or elsewhere the source of any information procured or obtained in the course of his employment or representation of such newspaper, press association, radio station or television station, whether published or not published in the newspaper or by the press association or broadcast or not broadcast by the radio station or television by which he is employed.

KENTUCKY—Rev. Stat. Ann. § 421.100 (1960):

421.100 [1649 d-1] *Newspaper, radio or television broadcasting station personnel need not disclose source of information.* No person shall be compelled to disclose in any legal proceeding or trial before any court, or before any grand or petit jury, or before the presiding officer of any tribunal, or his agent or agents, or before the General Assembly, or any committee thereof, or before any city or county legislative body, or any committee thereof, or elsewhere, the source of any information procured or obtained by him, and published in a newspaper or by a radio or television broadcasting station by which he is engaged or employed, or with which he is connected.

LOUISIANA—Rev. Stat. title 45 § 1451-54 (Supp. 1970):

§ 1451. *Definitions.* "Reporters" shall mean any person regularly engaged in the business of collecting, writing or editing news for publication through a news medium. The term reporter shall include all persons who were previously connected with any news media as aforesaid as to the information obtained while so connected. "News Media" shall include (a) Any newspaper or other periodical issued at regular intervals and having a paid general circulation; (b) Press associations: (c) Wire service; (d) Radio; (e) Television; and (f) Persons or corporations engaged in the making of news reels or other motion picture news for public showing.

§ 1452. *Conditional privilege from compulsory disclosure of informant or source.* Except as hereinafter provided, no reporter shall be compelled to disclose in any administrative, judicial or legislative proceedings or anywhere else the identity of any informant or any source of information obtained by him from another person while acting as a reporter.

§ 1453. *Revocation of privilege; procedure.* In any case where the reporter claims the privilege conferred by this Part, the persons or parties seeking the information may apply to the district court of the parish in which the reporter resides for an order to revoke the privilege. In the event the reporter does not reside within the state, the application shall be made to the district court of the parish where the hearing, action of proceeding in which the information is sought is pending. The application for such an order shall set forth in writing the reason why the disclosure is essential to the protection of the public interest and service of such application shall be made upon the reporter. The order shall be granted only when the court, after hearing the parties, shall find that the disclosure is essential to the public interest. Any such order shall be appealable under Article 2083 of the Louisiana Code of Civil Procedure. In case of any such appeal, the privilege set forth in R.S. 45:1452 shall remain in full force and effect during pendency of such appeal.

§ 1454. *Defamation; burden of proof.* If the privilege granted herein is claimed and if, in a suit for damages for defamation, a legal defense of good faith has been asserted by a reporter or by a news medium with respect to an issue upon which the reporter alleges to have obtained information from a confidential source, the burden of proof shall rest on the reporter or news medium to sustain this defense.

MARYLAND—Code Ann. article 35 § 2 (1965):

§ 2. *Employees on newspapers or for radio or television stations cannot be compelled to disclose source of news or information.* No person engaged in, connected with or employed on a newspaper or journal or for any radio or television station shall be compelled to disclose, in any legal proceeding or trial or before any committee of the legislature or elsewhere, the source of any news or information procured or obtained by him or published in the newspaper or disseminated by the radio or television station on and in which he is engaged, connected with or employed.

MICHIGAN—C.L. § 767.5a (1968):

767.5a *Certain communications declared privileged and confidential.* In any inquiry authorized by this act communications between reporters of newspapers or other publications and their informants are hereby declared to be privileged and confidential. Any communications between attorneys and their clients, between clergymen and the members of their respective churches, and between physicians and their patients are hereby declared to be privileged and confidential when such communications were necessary to enable such attorneys, clergymen, or physicians to serve as such attorney, clergyman, or physician.

MONTANA—R. Code Ann. title 93 § § 601-1, 601-2 (1947):

93-601-1. *Reporters' Confidence Act.* This act shall be known and may be cited as the Reporters' Confidence Act.

93-601-2. *Disclosure of source of information—when not required.* No persons engaged in the work of, or connected with or employed by any newspaper or any press association, or any radio broadcasting station, or any television station for the purpose of gathering, procuring, compiling, editing, disseminating, publishing, broadcasting or televising news shall be required to disclose the source of any information procured or obtained by such person in the course of his employment, in any legal proceeding, trial or investigation before any court, grand jury or petit jury, or any officer thereof, before the presiding officer of any tribunal, or his agent or agents, or before any commission, department, division or bureau of the state, or before any county or municipal body, officer or committee thereof.

NEW JERSEY—Rev. Stat. § 2A:84A-21 (Supp. 1970):

2A:84A-21. *Newspaperman's privilege.* Rule 27. Subject to Rule 37, a person engaged on, connected with, or employed by a newspaper has a privilege to refuse to disclose the source, author, means, agency or person from or through whom any information published in such newspaper was procured, obtained, supplied, furnished, or delivered.

[Rule 37: A person waives his right or privilege to refuse to disclose or to prevent another from disclosing a specified matter if he or any other person while the holder thereof has (a) contracted with anyone not to claim the right or privilege or, (b) without coercion and with knowledge of his right or privilege, made disclosure of any part of the privileged matter or consented to such a disclosure made by anyone.

A disclosure which is itself privileged or otherwise protected by the common law, statutes or rules of court of this State, or by lawful contract, shall not constitute a waiver under this section. The failure of a witness to claim a right or privilege with respect to one question shall not operate as a waiver with respect to any other question.]

NEW MEXICO—Stat. Ann. § 20-1-12.1 (Supp. 1970):

20-1-12.1 *Privileged communication—Reporters.* A. It is hereby declared to be the public policy of New Mexico that no reporter shall be required to disclose before any proceeding or by any authority the source of information procured by him in the course of his employment as a reporter for a news media unless disclosure be essential to prevent injustice. In granting or denying a testimonial privilege under this act [section], the court shall have due regard to the nature of the proceeding, the merits of the claim or defense, the adequacy of the remedy otherwise available, the relevancy of the source, and the possibility of establishing by other means that which the source is offered as tending to prove. An order compelling disclosure shall be appealable, and subject to stay.

B. As used in this section: (1) "reporter" means any person regularly engaged in the business of collecting, writing or editing news for publication through a news medium, and includes any person who was a reporter at the time the information was obtained but is no longer acting as a reporter; and (2) "news media" means any newspaper or other periodical issued at regular intervals and having a paid general circulation; a press association; a wire service; a radio station or a television station.

C. Any reporter may waive the privilege granted in this section.

NEW YORK—Civ. Rights Law § 79-h (McKinley 1970):

§ 79-h. Special provisions relating to persons employed by, or connected with, news media. (a) *Definitions.* As used in this section, the following definitions shall apply:

(1) "Newspaper" shall mean a paper that is printed and distributed ordinarily not less frequently than once a week, and has done so far at least one year, and that contains news, articles of opinion (as editorials), features, advertising, or other matter regarded as of current interest, has a paid circulation and has been entered at United States post office as second-class matter.

(2) "Magazine" shall mean a publication containing news which is published and distributed periodically, and has done so for at least one year, has a paid circulation and has been entered at a United States post office as second-class matter.

(3) "News agency" shall mean a commercial organization that collects and supplies news to subscribing newspapers, magazines, periodicals and news broadcasters.

(4) "Press association" shall mean an association of newspapers and/or magazines formed to gather and distribute news to its members.

(5) "Wire service" shall mean a news agency that sends out syndicated news copy by wire to subscribing newspapers, magazines, periodicals or news broadcasters.

(6) "Professional journalist" shall mean one who, for gain or livelihood, is engaged in gathering, preparing or editing of news for a newspaper, magazine, news agency, press association or wire service.

(7) "Newscaster" shall mean a person who, for gain or livelihood, is engaged in analyzing, commenting on or broadcasting, news by radio or television transmission.

(8) "News" shall mean written, oral or pictorial information or communication concerning local, national or worldwide events or other matters of public concern or public interest or affecting the public welfare.

(b) *Exemption of professional journalists and newscasters from contempt.* Notwithstanding the provisions of any general or specific law to the contrary, no professional journalist or newscaster employed or otherwise associated with any newspaper, magazine, news agency, press association, wire service, radio or television transmission station or network, shall be adjudged in contempt by any court, the legislature or other body having contempt powers, for refusing or failing to disclose any news or the source of any such news coming into his possession in the course of gathering or obtaining news for publication or to be published in a newspaper, magazine, or for broadcast by a radio or television transmission station or network, by which he is professionally employed or otherwise associated in a news gathering capacity.

NEVADA—Rev. Stat. § 48.087 (1969):

Section 48.087. No reporter or editorial employee of any newspaper, periodical, press association or radio or television station may be required to disclose the source of any information procured or obtained by such person, in any legal proceedings, trial or investigation:

1. Before any court, grand jury, coroner's inquest, jury or any office thereof.

2. Before the legislature of any committee thereof.

3. Before any department, agency or commission of the state.

4. Before any local governing body or committee thereof, or any officer of a local government.

OHIO—Rev. Code Ann. § § 2739.04,-.12

§ 2739.04 *Revelation of news source by broadcasters.* No person engaged in the work of, or connected with, or employed by any commercial radio broadcasting station, or any commercial television broadcasting station, or network of such stations, for the purpose of gathering, procuring, compiling, editing, disseminating, publishing or broadcasting news shall be required to disclose the source of any information procured or obtained by such person in the course of his employment, in any legal proceeding, trial, or investigation before any court, grand jury, petit jury, or any officer thereof, before the presiding officer of any tribunal, or his agent, or before any commission, department, division, or bureau of this state, or before any county or municipal body, officer or committee thereof.

Every commercial radio broadcasting station, and every commercial television broadcasting station shall maintain for a period of six months from the date of its broadcast thereof, a record of those statements of information the source of which was procured or obtained by persons employed by the station in gathering, procuring, compiling, editing, disseminating, publishing, or broadcasting news.

§ 2739.12 *Newspaper reporters not required to reveal source of information.* (GC § 6319-2a) No person engaged in the work of, or connected with, or employed by any newspaper or any press association for the purpose of gathering, procuring, compiling, editing, disseminating, or publishing news shall be required to disclose the source of any information procured or obtained by such person in the course of his employment, in any legal proceeding, trial, or investigation before any court, grand jury, petit jury, or any officer thereof, before the presiding officer of any tribunal, or his agent, or before any commission, department, division, or bureau of this state, or before any county or municipal body, officer or committee thereof.

PENNSYLVANIA—Stat. Ann. title 28 § 330 (1958):

§ 330. *Confidential communications to news reporters.* (a) No person, engaged on, connected with, or employed by any newspaper of general circulation as defined by the laws of this Commonwealth, or any press association or any radio or television station, or any magazine of general circulation, for the purpose of gathering, procuring, compiling, editing or publishing news, shall be required to disclose the source of any information procured or obtained by such person, in any legal proceeding, trial or investigation before any court, grand jury, traverse or petit jury, or any officer thereof, before the General Assembly or any committee thereof, before any commission, department or bureau of this Commonwealth, or before any county or municipal body, officer, or committee thereof.

(b) The provisions of subsection (a) hereof in so far as they relate to radio or television stations will not apply unless the radio or television station maintains and keeps open for inspection, for a period of at least one year from the date of the actual broadcast or telecast, an exact recording, transcription, kinescopic film or certified written transcript of the actual broadcast or telecast.

Appendix 2

Department of Justice Guidelines for Subpoenas to the News Media

1. The Department of Justice recognizes that compulsory process in some circumstances may have a limiting effect on the exercise of First Amendment rights. In determining whether to request issuance of a subpoena to the press, the approach in every case must be to weigh that limiting effect against the public interest to be served in the fair administration of justice.

2. The Department of Justice does not consider the press "an investigative arm of the government." Therefore, all reasonable attempts should be made to obtain information from non-press sources before there is any consideration of subpoenaing the press.

3. It is the policy of the Department to insist that negotiations with the press be attempted in all cases in which a subpoena is contemplated. These negotiations should attempt to accommodate the interests of the grand jury with the interests of the news media.

   In these negotiations, where the nature of the investigation permits, the government should make clear what its needs are in a particular case as well as its willingness to respond to particular problems of the news media.

4. If negotiations fail, no Justice Department official should request, or make any arrangements for, a subpoena to the press without the express authorization of the Attorney General.

   If a subpoena is obtained under such circumstances without this authorization, the Department will—as a matter of course—move to quash the subpoena without prejudice to its rights subsequently to request the subpoena upon the proper authorization.

5. In requesting the Attorney General's authorization for a subpoena, the following principles will apply:

   A. There should be sufficient reason to believe that a crime has occurred, from disclosures by non-press sources. The Department does not approve of utilizing the press as a spring board for investigations.

   B. There should be sufficient reason to believe that the information sought is essential to a successful investigation—particularly with reference to directly establishing guilt or innocence. The subpoena should not be used to obtain peripheral, non-essential or speculative information.

   C. The government should have unsuccessfully attempted to obtain the information from alternative non-press sources.

   D. Authorization requests for subpoenas should normally be limited to the verification of published information and to such surrounding circumstances as relate to the accuracy of the published information.

   E. Great caution should be observed in requesting subpoena authorization by the Attorney General for unpublished information, or where an orthodox First Amendment defense is raised or where a serious claim of confidentiality is alleged.

   F. Even subpoena authorization requests for publicly disclosed information should be treated with care because, for example, cameramen have recently been subjected to harassment on the grounds that their photographs will become available to the government.

G. In any event, subpoenas should, wherever possible, be directed at material information regarding a limited subject matter, should cover a reasonably limited period of time, and should avoid requiring production of a large volume of unpublished material. They should give reasonable and timely notice of the demand for documents.

These are general rules designed to cover the great majority of cases. It must always be remembered that emergencies and other unusual situations may develop where a subpoena request to the Attorney General may be submitted which does not exactly conform to these guidelines.

SUPREME COURT OF THE UNITED STATES

Nos. 1873 AND 1885.—OCTOBER TERM, 1970

New York Times Company, Petitioner, 1873 *v.* United States.

On Writ of Certiorari to the United States Court of Appeals for the Second Circuit.

United States, Petitioner, 1885 *v.* The Washington Post Company et al.

On Writ of Certiorari to the United States Court of Appeals for the District of Columbia Circuit.

[June 30, 1971]

PER CURIAM.

We granted certiorari in these cases in which the United States seeks to enjoin the New York Times and the Washington Post from publishing the contents of a classified study entitled "History of U. S. Decision-Making Process on Viet Nam Policy." — U. S. — (1971).

"Any system of prior restraints of expression comes to this Court bearing a heavy presumption against its constitutional validity." *Bantam Books, Inc.* v. *Sullivan,* 372 U. S. 58, 70 (1963); see also *Near* v. *Minnesota,* 283 U. S. 697 (1931). The Government "thus carries a heavy burden of showing justification for the enforcement of such a restraint." *Organization for a Better Austin* v. *Keefe,* — U. S. — (1971). The District Court for the Southern District of New York in the *New York Times* case and the District Court for the District of Columbia and the Court of Appeals for the District of Columbia Circuit in the *Washington Post* case held that the Government had not met that burden. We agree.

The judgment of the Court of Appeals for the District of Columbia Circuit is therefore affirmed.   The order of the Court of Appeals for the Second Circuit is reversed and the case is remanded with directions to enter a judgment affirming the judgment of the District Court for the Southern District of New York.   The stays entered June 25, 1971, by the Court are vacated.   The judgments shall issue forthwith.

So ordered.

SUPREME COURT OF THE UNITED STATES

Nos. 1873 AND 1885.—OCTOBER TERM, 1970

New York Times Company, Petitioner, 1873 v. United States.	On Writ of Certiorari to the United States Court of Appeals for the Second Circuit.

United States, Petitioner, 1885 v. The Washington Post Company et al.	On Writ of Certiorari to the United States Court of Appeals for the District of Columbia Circuit.

[June 30, 1971]

MR. JUSTICE BLACK, with whom MR. JUSTICE DOUGLAS joins, concurring.

I adhere to the view that the Government's case against the Washington Post should have been dismissed and that the injunction against the New York Times should have been vacated without oral argument when the cases were first presented to this Court. I believe that every moment's continuance of the injunctions against these newspapers amounts to a flagrant, indefensible, and continuing violation of the First Amendment. Furthermore, after oral arguments, I agree completely that we must affirm the judgment of the Court of Appeals for the District of Columbia and reverse the judgment of the Court of Appeals for the Second Circuit for the reasons stated by my Brothers DOUGLAS and BRENNAN. In my view it is unfortunate that some of my Brethren are apparently willing to hold that the publication of news may sometimes be enjoined. Such a holding would make a shambles of the First Amendment.

Our Government was launched in 1789 with the adoption of the Constitution. The Bill of Rights, including the First Amendment, followed in 1791. Now, for the first time in the 182 years since the founding of the Republic, the federal courts are asked to hold that the First Amendment does not mean what it says, but rather means that the Government can halt the publication of current news of vital importance to the people of this country.

In seeking injunctions against these newspapers and in its presentation to the Court, the Executive Branch seems to have forgotten the essential purpose and history of the First Amendment. When the Constitution was adopted, many people strongly opposed it because the document contained no Bill of Rights to safeguard certain basic freedoms.[1] They especially feared that the new powers granted to a central government might be interpreted to permit the government to curtail freedom of religion, press, assembly, and speech. In response to an overwhelming public clamor, James Madison offered a series of amendments to satisfy citizens that these great liberties would remain safe and beyond the power of government to abridge. Madison proposed what later became the First Amendment in three parts, two of which are set out below, and one of which proclaimed: "The people shall not be deprived or abridged of their right to speak, to write, or to publish their sentiments; *and the freedom of the press, as one of the great bul-*

---

[1] In introducing the Bill of Rights in the House of Representatives, Madison said: "[B]ut I believe that the great mass of the people who opposed [the Constitution], disliked it because it did not contain effectual provisions against the encroachments on particular rights . . . ." 1 Annals of Congress 433 (1834). Congressman Goodhue added: "[I]t is the wish of many of our constituents, that something should be added to the Constitution, to secure in a stronger manner their liberties from the inroads of power." *Id.,* at 426.

warks of liberty, shall be inviolable." [2]   The amendments were offered to *curtail* and *restrict* the general powers granted to the Executive, Legislative, and Judicial Branches two years before in the original Constitution. The Bill of Rights changed the original Constitution into a new charter under which no branch of government could abridge the people's freedoms of press, speech, religion, and assembly.   Yet the Solicitor General argues and some members of the Court appear to agree that the general powers of the Government adopted in the original Constitution should be interpreted to limit and restrict the specific and emphatic guarantees of the Bill of Rights adopted later.   I can imagine no greater perversion of history.   Madison and the other Framers of the First Amendment, able men that they were, wrote in language they earnestly believed could never be misunderstood: "Congress shall make no law . . . abridging the freedom of the press . . . ."   Both the history and language of the First Amendment support the view that the press must be left free to publish news, whatever the source, without censorship, injunctions, or prior restraints.

In the First Amendment the Founding Fathers gave the free press the protection it must have to fulfill its essential role in our democracy.   The press was to serve the governed, not the governors.   The Government's power to censor the press was abolished so that the press would remain forever free to censure the Govern-

---

[2] The other parts were:

"The civil rights of none shall be abridged on account of religious belief or worship, nor shall any national religion be established, nor shall the full and equal rights of conscience be in any manner, or on any pretext, infringed.

"The people shall not be restrained from peaceably assembling and consulting for their common good; nor from applying to the Legislature by petitions, or remonstrances, for redress of their grievances." 1 Annals of Congress 434 (1834).   (Emphasis added.)

ment. The press was protected so that it could bare the secrets of government and inform the people. Only a free and unrestrained press can effectively expose deception in government. And paramount among the responsibilities of a free press is the duty to prevent any part of the government from deceiving the people and sending them off to distant lands to die of foreign fevers and foreign shot and shell. In my view, far from deserving condemnation for their courageous reporting, the New York Times, the Washington Post, and other newspapers should be commended for serving the purpose that the Founding Fathers saw so clearly. In revealing the workings of government that led to the Viet Nam war, the newspapers nobly did precisely that which the Founders hoped and trusted they would do.

The Government's case here is based on premises entirely different from those that guided the Framers of the First Amendment. The Solicitor General has carefully and emphatically stated:

"Now, Mr. Justice [BLACK], your construction of . . . [the First Amendment] is well known, and I certainly respect it. You say that no law means no law, and that should be obvious. I can only say, Mr Justice that to me it is equally obvious that 'no law' does not mean 'no law', and I would seek to persuade the Court that that is true. . . . [T]here are other parts of the Constitution that grant power and responsibilities to the Executive and . . . the First Amendment was not intended to make it impossible for the Executive to function or to protect the security of the United States." [3]

And the Government argues in its brief that in spite of the First Amendment, "[t]he authority of the Executive Department to protect the nation against publica-

[3] Transcript of Oral Argument, at 76.

tion of information whose disclosure would endanger the national security stems from two interrelated sources: the constitutional power of the President over the conduct of foreign affairs and his authority as Commander-in-Chief." [4]

In other words, we are asked to hold that despite the First Amendment's emphatic command, the Executive Branch, the Congress, and the Judiciary can make laws enjoining publication of current news and abridging freedom of the press in the name of "national security." The Government does not even attempt to rely on any act of Congress. Instead it makes the bold and dangerously far-reaching contention that the courts should take it upon themselves to "make" a law abridging freedom of the press in the name of equity, presidential power and national security, even when the representatives of the people in Congress have adhered to the command of the First Amendment and refused to make such a law.[5] See concurring opinion of MR. JUSTICE DOUGLAS, *post,* at ——. To find that the President has "inherent power" to halt the publication of news by resort to the courts would wipe out the First Amendment and destroy the fundamental liberty and security of the very people the Government hopes to make "secure." No one can read the history of the adoption of the First Amendment without being convinced beyond any doubt that it was

---

[4] Brief for United States, at 12.

[5] Compare the views of the Solicitor General with those of James Madison, the author of the First Amendment. When speaking of the Bill of Rights in the House of Representatives, Madison said: "If they [the first ten amendments] are incorporated into the Constitution, independent tribunals of justice will consider themselves in a peculiar manner the guardians of those rights; they will be an impenetrable bulwark against every assumption of power in the Legislative or Executive; they will be naturally led to resist every encroachment upon rights expressly stipulated for in the Constitution by the declaration of rights." 1 Annals of Congress 439 (1834).

injunctions like those sought here that Madison and his collaborators intended to outlaw in this Nation for all time.

The word "security" is a broad, vague generality whose contours should not be invoked to abrogate the fundamental law embodied in the First Amendment. The guarding of military and diplomatic secrets at the expense of informed representative government provides no real security for our Republic. The Framers of the First Amendment, fully aware of both the need to defend a new nation and the abuses of the English and Colonial governments, sought to give this new society strength and security by providing that freedom of speech, press, religion, and assembly should not be abridged. This thought was eloquently expressed in 1937 by Mr. Chief Justice Hughes—great man and great Chief Justice that he was—when the Court held a man could not be punished for attending a meeting run by Communists.

> "The greater the importance of safeguarding the community from incitements to the overthrow of our institutions by force and violence, the more imperative is the need to preserve inviolate the constitutional rights of free speech, free press and free assembly in order to maintain the opportunity for free political discussion, to the end that government may be responsive to the will of the people and that changes, if desired, may be obtained by peaceful means. Therein lies the security of the Republic, the very foundation of constitutional government." [6]

---

[6] *DeJonge* v. *Oregon,* 299 U. S. 353, 365 (1937).

SUPREME COURT OF THE UNITED STATES

Nos. 1873 AND 1885.—OCTOBER TERM, 1970

New York Times Company, Petitioner, 1873 *v.* United States.	On Writ of Certiorari to the United States Court of Appeals for the Second Circuit.
United States, Petitioner, 1885 *v.* The Washington Post Company et al.	On Writ of Certiorari to the United States Court of Appeals for the District of Columbia Circuit.

[June 30, 1971]

MR. JUSTICE DOUGLAS, with whom MR. JUSTICE BLACK joins, concurring.

While I join the opinion of the Court I believe it necessary to express my views more fully.

It should be noted at the ouset that the First Amendment provides that "Congress shall make no law . . . abridging the freedom of speech or of the press." That leaves, in my view, no room for governmental restraint on the press.[1]

There is, moreover, no statute barring the publication by the press of the material which the Times and Post seek to use. 18 U. S. C. § 793 (e) provides that "whoever having unauthorized possession of, access to, or control over any document, writing, . . . or information relating to the national defense which information the possessor

---

[1] See *Beauharnais* v. *Illinois*, 343 U. S. 250, 267 (dissenting opinion of MR. JUSTICE BLACK), 284 (my dissenting opinion); *Roth* v. *United States*, 354 U. S. 476, 508 (my dissenting opinion which MR. JUSTICE BLACK joined); *Yates* v. *United States*, 354 U. S. 298, 339 (separate opinion of MR. JUSTICE BLACK which I joined); *New York Times* v. *Sullivan*, 376 U. S. 254, 293 (concurring opinion of MR. JUSTICE BLACK which I joined); *Garrison* v. *Louisiana*, 379 U. S. 64, 80 (my concurring opinion which MR. JUSTICE BLACK joined).

has reason to believe could be used to the injury of the United States or to the advantage of any foreign nation, wilfully communicates . . . the same to any person not entitled to receive it . . . shall be fined not more than $10,000 or imprisoned not more than ten years or both."

The Government suggests that the word "communicates" is broad enough to encompass publication.

There are eight sections in the chapter on espionage and censorship, §§ 792–799. In three of those eight "publish" is specifically mentioned: § 794 (b) provides "Whoever in time of war, with the intent that the same shall be communicated to the enemy, collects records, *publishes,* or communicates . . . [the disposition of armed forces]."

Section 797 prohibits "reproduces, *publishes,* sells, or gives away" photos of defense installations.

Section 798 relating to cryptography prohibits: "communicates, furnishes, transmits, or otherwise makes available . . . *or publishes.*" [2]

Thus it is apparent that Congress was capable of and did distinguish between publishing and communication in the various sections of the Espionage Act.

The other evidence that § 793 does not apply to the press is a rejected version of § 793. That version read: "During any national emergency resulting from a war to which the U. S. is a party or from threat of such a war, the President may, by proclamation, prohibit the publishing or communicating of, or the attempting to publish or communicate any information relating to the national defense, which in his judgment is of such character that it is or might be useful to the enemy." During

---

[2] These papers contain data concerning the communications system of the United States, the publication of which is made a crime. But the criminal sanction is not urged by the United States as the basis of equity power.

the debates in the Senate the First Amendment was specifically cited and that provision was defeated. 55 Cong Rec. 2166.

Judge Gurfein's holding in the *Times* case that this Act does not apply to this case was therefore pre-eminently sound. Moreover, the Act of September 23, 1950, in amending 18 U. S. C. § 793 states in § 1 (b) that:

> "Nothing in this Act shall be construed to author-ize, require, or establish military or civilian censor-ship or in any way to limit or infringe upon freedom of the press or of speech as guaranteed by the Con-stitution of the United States and no regulation shall be promulgated hereunder having that effect." 64 Stat. 987.

Thus Congress has been faithful to the command of the First Amendment in this area.

So any power that the Government possesses must come from its "inherent power."

The power to wage war is "the power to wage war suc-cessfully." See *Hirabayashi* v. *United States,* 320 U. S. 81, 93. But the war power stems from a declaration of war. The Constitution by Article I, § 8, gives Con-gress, not the President, power "to declare war." No-where are presidential wars authorized. We need not decide therefore what leveling effect the war power of Congress might have.

These disclosures [3] may have a serious impact. But that is no basis for sanctioning a previous restraint on

---

[3] There are numerous sets of this material in existence and they apparently are not under any controlled custody. Moreover, the President has sent a set to the Congress. We start then with a case where there already is rather wide distribution of the material that is destined for publicity, not secrecy. I have gone over the material listed in the *in camera* brief of the United States. It is all history, not future events. None of it is more recent than 1968.

the press.   As stated by Chief Justice Hughes in *Near v. Minnesota,* 283 U. S. 697, 719–720:

> ". . . While reckless assaults upon public men, and efforts to bring obloquy upon those who are endeavoring faithfully to discharge official duties, exert a baleful influence and deserve the severest condemnation in public opinion, it cannot be said that this abuse is greater, and it is believed to be less, than that which characterized the period in which our institutions took shape.   Meanwhile, the administration of government has become more complex, the opportunities for malfeasance and corruption have multiplied, crime has grown to most serious proportions, and the danger of its protection by unfaithful officials and of the impairment of the fundamental security of life and property by criminal alliances and official neglect, emphasizes the primary need of a vigilant and courageous press, especially in great cities.   The fact that the liberty of the press may be abused by miscreant purveyors of scandal does not make any the less necessary the immunity of the press from previous restraint in dealing with official misconduct."

As we stated only the other day in *Organization for a Better Austin* v. *Keefe,* —— U. S. ——, "any prior restraint on expression comes to this Court with a 'heavy presumption' against its constitutional validity."

The Government says that it has inherent powers to go into court and obtain an injunction to protect that national interest, which in this case is alleged to be national security.

Near v. *Minnesota,* 283 U. S. 697, repudiated that expansive doctrine in no uncertain terms.

The dominant purpose of the First Amendment was to prohibit the widespread practice of governmental suppression of embarrassing information.   It is common knowledge that the First Amendment was adopted against the widespread use of the common law of seditious libel to punish the dissemination of material that is embarassing to the powers-that-be.   See Emerson, The System of Free Expressions, c. V (1970); Chafee, Free Speech in the United States, c. XIII (1941).   The present cases will, I think, go down in history as the most dramatic illustration of that principle.   A debate of large proportions goes on in the Nation over our posture in Vietnam. That debate antedated the disclosure of the contents of the present documents.   The latter are highly relevant to the debate in progress.

Secrecy in government is fundamentally anti-democratic, perpetuating bureaucratic errors.   Open debate and discussion of public issues are vital to our national health.   On public questions there should be "open and robust debate."   *New York Times, Inc.* v. *Sullivan,* 376 U. S. 254, 269–270.

I would affirm the judgment of the Court of Appeals in the *Post* case, vacate the stay of the Court of Appeals in the *Times* case and direct that it affirm the District Court.

The stays in these cases that have been in effect for more than a week constitute a flouting of the principles of the First Amendment as interpreted in *Near* v. *Minnesota.*

SUPREME COURT OF THE UNITED STATES

Nos. 1873 AND 1885.—OCTOBER TERM, 1970

| New York Times Company, Petitioner, 1873 v. United States. | On Writ of Certiorari to the United States Court of Appeals for the Second Circuit. |

| United States, Petitioner, 1885 v. The Washington Post Company et al. | On Writ of Certiorari to the United States Court of Appeals for the District of Columbia Circuit. |

[June 30, 1971]

MR. JUSTICE BRENNAN, concurring.

I

I write separately in these cases only to emphasize what should be apparent: that our judgment in the present cases may not be taken to indicate the propriety, in the future, of issuing temporary stays and restraining orders to block the publication of material sought to be suppressed by the Government. So far as I can determine, never before has the United States sought to enjoin a newspaper from publishing information in its possession. The relative novelty of the questions presented, the necessary haste with which decisions were reached, the magnitude of the interests asserted, and the fact that all the parties have concentrated their arguments upon the question whether permanent restraints were proper may have justified at least some of the restraints heretofore imposed in these cases. Certainly it is difficult to fault the several courts below for seeking to asure that the issues here involved were preserved for ultimate review by this Court. But even if it be assumed that some of the interim restraints were proper in the two cases before us, that assumption has no bearing upon the propriety of similar judicial action in the future. To begin with, there has now been ample time for reflection and judgment; whatever values there may be in the preservation of novel questions for appellate review may not support any restraints in the future. More important, the First Amendment stands as an absolute bar to the imposition of judicial restraints in circumstances of the kind presented by these cases.

II

The error which has pervaded these cases from the outset was the granting of any injunctive relief whatsoever, interim or otherwise. The entire thrust of the Government's claim throughout these cases has been that publication of the material sought to be enjoined "could," or "might," or "may" prejudice the national interest in various ways. But the First Amendment tolerates absolutely no prior judicial restraints of the press predicated upon surmise or conjecture that untoward consequences may result.* Our cases, it is true, have indicated that there is a single, extremely narrow class of cases in which the First Amendment's ban on prior judicial restraint

---

Freedman v. *Maryland,* 380 U. S. 51 (1965), and similar cases regarding temporary restraints of allegedly obscene materials are not in point. For those cases rest upon the proposition that "obscenity is not protected by the freedoms of speech and press." *Roth* v. *United States,* 354 U. S. 476 (1957). Here there is no question but that the material sought to be suppressed is within the protection of the First Amendment; the only question is whether, notwithstanding that fact, its publication may be enjoined for a time because of the presence of an overwhelming national interest. Similarly, copyright cases have no pertinence here: the Government is not asserting an interest in the particular form of words chosen in the documents, but is seeking to suppress the ideas expressed therein. And the copyright laws, of course, protect only the form of expression and not the ideas expressed.

may be overridden. Our cases have thus far indicated that such cases may arise only when the Nation "is at war," *Schenck* v. *United States,* 249 U. S. 47, 52 (1919), during which times "no one would question but that a Government might prevent actual obstruction to its recruiting service or the publication of the sailing dates of transports or the number and location of troops." *Near* v. *Minnesota,* 283 U. S. 697, 716 (1931). Even if the present world situation were assumed to be tantamount to a time of war, or if the power of presently available armaments would justify even in peacetime the suppression of information that would set in motion a nuclear holocaust, in neither of these actions has the Government presented or even alleged that publication of items from or based upon the material at issue would cause the happening of an event of that nature. "The chief purpose of [the First Amendment's] guarantee [is] to prevent previous restraints upon publication." *Near* v *Minnesota, supra,* at 713. Thus, only governmental allegation and proof that publication must inevitably, directly and immediately cause the occurrence of an event kindred to imperiling the safety of a transport already at sea can support even the issuance of an interim restraining order. In no event may mere conclusions be sufficient: for if the Executive Branch seeks judicial aid in preventing publication, it must inevitably submit the basis upon which that aid is sought to scrutiny by the judiciary. And therefore, every restraint issued in this case, whatever its form, has violated the First Amendment—and none the less so because that restraint was justified as necessary to afford the court an opportunity to examine the claim more thoroughly. Unless and until the Government has clearly made out its case, the First Amendment commands that no injunction may issue.

SUPREME COURT OF THE UNITED STATES

Nos. 1873 AND 1885.—OCTOBER TERM, 1970

New York Times Company, Petitioner, 1873 v. United States.

On Writ of Certiorari to the United States Court of Appeals for the Second Circuit.

United States, Petitioner, 1885 v. The Washington Post Company et al.

On Writ of Certiorari to the United States Court of Appeals for the District of Columbia Circuit.

[June 30, 1971]

MR. JUSTICE STEWART, with whom MR. JUSTICE WHITE joins, concurring.

In the governmental structure created by our Constitution, the Executive is endowed with enormous power in the two related areas of national defense and international relations. This power, largely unchecked by the Legislative[1] and Judicial[2] branches, has been pressed to the very hilt since the advent of the nuclear missile

---

[1] The President's power to make treaties and to appoint ambassadors is of course limited by the requirement of Article II, § 1, of the Constitution that he obtain the advice and consent of the Senate. Article I, § 8, empowers Congress to "raise and support Armies," and "provide and maintain a Navy." And, of course, Congress alone can declare war. This power was last exercised almost 30 years ago at the inception of World War II. Since the end of that war in 1945, the Armed Forces of the United States have suffered approximately half a million casualties in various parts of the world.

[2] See *Chicago & Southern Air Lines* v. *Waterman Steamship Corp.*, 333 U. S. 103; *Hirabayashi* v. *United States*, 320 U. S. 81; *United States* v. *Curtiss-Wright Export Corp.*, 299 U. S. 304; cf. *Mora* v. *McNamara*, cert. denied 389 U. S. 934.

age. For better or for worse, the simple fact is that a President of the United States possesses vastly greater constitutional independence in these two vital areas of power than does, say, a prime minister of a country with a parliamentary form of government.

In the absence of the governmental checks and balances present in other areas of our national life, the only effective restraint upon executive policy and power in the areas of national defense and international affairs may lie in an enlightened citizenry—in an informed and critical public opinion which alone can here protect the values of democratic government. For this reason, it is perhaps here that a press that is alert, aware, and free most vitally serves the basic purpose of the First Amendment. For without an informed and free press there cannot be an enlightened people.

Yet it is elementary that the successful conduct of international diplomacy and the maintenance of an effective national defense require both confidentiality and secrecy. Other nations can hardly deal with this Nation in an atmosphere of mutual trust unless they can be assured that their confidences will be kept. And within our own executive departments, the development of considered and intelligent international policies would be impossible if those charged with their formulation could not communicate with each other freely, frankly, and in confidence. In the area of basic national defense the frequent need for absolute secrecy is, of course, self-evident.

I think there can be but one answer to this dilemma, if dilemma it be. The responsibility must be where the power is.[3] If the Constitution gives the Executive

---

[3] "It is quite apparent that if, in the maintenance of our international relations, embarrassment—perhaps serious embarrassment—is to be avoided and success for our aims achieved, congressional legislation which is to be made effective through negotiation and inquiry within the international field must often accord to the President a

a large degree of unshared power in the conduct of foreign affairs and the maintenance of our national defense, then under the Constitution the Executive must have the largely unshared duty to determine and preserve the degree of internal security necessary to exercise that power successfully.   It is an awesome responsibility, requiring judgment and wisdom of a high order. I should suppose that moral, political, and practical considerations would dictate that a very first principle of that wisdom would be an insistence upon avoiding secrecy for its own sake.   For when everything is classified, then nothing is classified, and the system becomes one to be disregarded by the cynical or the careless, and to be manipulated by those intent on self-protection or self-promotion.   I should suppose, in short, that the hallmark of a truly effective internal security system would be the maximum possible disclosure, recognizing that secrecy can best be preserved only when credibility is truly maintained.   But be that as it may, it is clear to me that it is the constitutional duty of the Executive— as a matter of sovereign perogative and not as a matter

---

degree of discretion and freedom from statutory restriction which would not be admissible were domestic affairs alone involved.   Moreover, he, not Congress, has the better opportunity of knowing the conditions which prevail in foreign countries, and especially is this true in time of war.   He has his confidential sources of information. He has his agents in the form of diplomatic, consular and other officials.   Secrecy in respect of information gathered by them may be highly necessary, and the premature disclosure of it productive of harmful results.   Indeed, so clearly is this true that the first President refused to accede to a request to lay before the House of Representatives the instructions, correspondence and documents relating to the negotiation of the Jay Treaty—a refusal the wisdom of which was recognized by the House itself and has never since been doubted. . . ." *United States* v. *Curtiss-Wright Corp.,* 299 U. S. 304, at 320.

of law as the courts know law—through the promulgation and enforcement of executive regulations, to protect the confidentiality necessary to carry out its responsibilities in the fields of international relations and national defense.

This is not to say that Congress and the courts have no role to play. Undoubtedly Congress has the power to enact specific and appropriate criminal laws to protect government property and preserve government secrets. Congress has passed such laws, and several of them are of very colorable relevance to the apparent circumstances of these cases. And if a criminal prosecution is instituted, it will be the responsibility of the courts to decide the applicability of the criminal law under which the charge is brought. Moreover, if Congress should pass a specific law authorizing civil proceedings in this field, the courts would likewise have the duty to decide the constitutionality of such a law as well as its applicability to the facts proved.

But in the cases before us we are asked neither to construe specific regulations nor to apply specific laws. We are asked, instead, to perform a function that the Constitution gave to the Executive, not the Judiciary. We are asked, quite simply, to prevent the publication by two newspapers of material that the Executive Branch insists should not, in the national interest, be published. I am convinced that the Executive is correct with respect to some of the documents involved. But I cannot say that disclosure of any of them will surely result in direct, immediate, and irreparable damage to our Nation or its people. That being so, there can under the First Amendment be but one judicial resolution of the issues before us. I join the judgments of the Court.

SUPREME COURT OF THE UNITED STATES

Nos. 1873 and 1885.—October Term, 1970

New York Times Company, Petitioner, 1873 v. United States.	On Writ of Certiorari to the United States Court of Appeals for the Second Circuit.

United States, Petitioner, 1885 v. The Washington Post Company et al.	On Writ of Certiorari to the United States Court of Appeals for the District of Columbia Circuit.

[June 30, 1971]

MR. JUSTICE WHITE, with whom MR. JUSTICE STEWART joins, concurring.

I concur in today's judgments, but only because of the concededly extraordinary protection against prior restraints enjoyed by the press under our constitutional system. I do not say that in no circumstances would the First Amendment permit an injunction against publishing information about government plans or operations.[1] Nor, after examining the materials the Govern-

---

[1] The Congress has authorized a strain of prior restraints against private parties in certain instances. The National Labor Relations Board routinely issues cease-and-desist orders against employers whom it finds have threatened or coerced employees in the exercise of protected rights. See 29 U. S. C. § 160 (c). Similarly, the Federal Trade Commission is empowered to impose cease-and-desist orders against unfair methods of competition. 15 U. S. C. § 45 (b). Such orders can, and quite often do, restrict what may be spoken or written under certain circumstances. See, *e. g.*, *NLRB* v. *Gissel Packing Co.*, 395 U. S. 575, 616–620 (1969). Art. I, § 8 of the Constitution authorizes Congress to secure the "exclusive right" of authors to their writings, and no one denies that a newspaper can properly be enjoined from publishing the copyrighted works of another. See *Westermann Co.* v. *Dispatch Co.*, 249 U. S. 100

ment characterizes as the most sensitive and destructive, can I deny that revelation of these documents will do substantial damage to public interests. Indeed, I am confident that their disclosure will have that result. But I nevertheless agree that the United States has not satisfied the very heavy burden which it must meet to warrant an injunction against publication in these cases, at least in the absence of express and appropriately limited congressional authorization for prior restraints in circumstances such as these.

The Government's position is simply stated: The responsibility of the Executive for the conduct of the foreign affairs and for the security of the Nation is so basic that the President is entitled to an injunction against publication of a newspaper story whenever he can convince a court that the information to be revealed threatens "grave and irreparable" injury to the public interest; [2] and the injunction should issue whether or not the material to be published is classified, whether or not publication would be lawful under relevant criminal statutes enacted

---

(1919). Newspapers do themselves rely from time to time on the copyright as a means of protecting their accounts of important events. However, those enjoined under the statutes relating to the National Labor Relations Board and the Federal Trade Commission are private parties, not the press; and when the press is enjoined under the copyright laws the complainant is a private copyright holder enforcing a private right. These situations are quite distinct from the Government's request for an injunction against publishing information about the affairs of government, a request admittedly not based on any statute.

[2] The "grave and irreparable danger" standard is that asserted by the Government in this Court. In remanding to Judge Gurfein for further hearings in the *Times* litigation, five members of the Court of Appeals for the Second Circuit directed him to determine whether disclosure of certain items specified with particularity by the Government would "pose such grave and immediate danger to the security of the United States as to warrant their publication being enjoined."

by Congress and regardless of the circumstances by which the newspaper came into possession of the information.

At least in the absence of legislation by Congress, based on its own investigations and findings, I am quite unable to agree that the inherent powers of the Executive and the courts reach so far as to authorize remedies having such sweeping potential for inhibiting publications by the press.   Much of the difficulty inheres in the "grave and irreparable danger" standard suggested by the United States.   If the United States were to have judgment under such a standard in these cases, our decision would be of little guidance to other courts in other cases, for the material at issue here would not be available from the Court's opinion or from public records, nor would it be published by the press.   Indeed, even today where we hold that the United States has not met its burden, the material remains sealed in court records and it is properly not discussed in today's opinions.   Moreover, because the material poses substantial dangers to national interests and because of the hazards of criminal sanctions, a responsible press may choose never to publish the more sensitive materials.   To sustain the Government in these cases would start the courts down a long and hazardous road that I am not willing to travel at least without congressional guidance and direction.

It is not easy to reject the proposition urged by the United States and to deny relief on its good-faith claims in these cases that publication will work serious damage to the country.   But that discomfiture is considerably dispelled by the infrequency of prior restraint cases. Normally, publication will occur and the damage be done before the Government has either opportunity or grounds for suppression.   So here, publication has already begun and a substantial part of the threatened damage has already occurred.   The fact of a massive breakdown in security is known, access to the documents by many unauthorized people is undeniable and the efficacy of equitable relief against these or other newspapers to avert anticipated damage is doubtful at best.

What is more, terminating the ban on publication of the relatively few sensitive documents the Government now seeks to suppress does not mean that the law either requires or invites newspapers or others to publish them or that they will be immune from criminal action if they do. Prior restraints require an unusually heavy justification under the First Amendment; but failure by the Government to justify prior restraints does not measure its constitutional entitlement to a conviction for criminal publication. That the Government mistakenly chose to proceed by injunction does not mean that it could not successfully proceed in another way.

When the Espionage Act was under consideration in 1917, Congress eliminated from the bill a provision that would have given the President broad powers in time of war to proscribe, under threat of criminal penalty, the publication of various categories of information related to the national defense.[3] Congress at that time was unwilling to clothe the President with such far-reaching powers to monitor the press, and those opposed to this part of the legislation assumed that a necessary concomitant of such power was the power to "filter out the news to the people through some man." 55 Cong. Rec.

---

[3] "Whoever, in time of war, in violation of reasonable regulations to be prescribed by the President, which he is hereby authorized to make and promulgate, shall publish any information with respect to the movement, numbers, description, condition, or disposition of any of the armed forces, ships, aircraft, or war materials of the United States, or with respect to the plans or conduct of any naval or military operations, or with respect to any works or measures undertaken for or connected with, or intended for the fortification or defense of any place, or any other information relating to the public defense calculated to be useful to the enemy, shall be punished by a fine . . . or by imprisonment . . . ." 55 Cong. Rec. 2100 (1917).

2008 (1917) (remarks of Senator Ashurst). However, these same members of Congress appeared to have little doubt that newspapers would be subject to criminal prosecution if they insisted on publishing information of the type Congress had itself determined should not be revealed. Senator Ashurst, for example, was quite sure that the editor of such a newspaper "should be punished if he did publish information as to the movements of the fleet, the troops, the aircraft, the location of powder factories, the location of defense works, and all that sort of thing." 55 Cong. Rec. 2009 (1917).[4]

The criminal code contains numerous provisions potentially relevant to these cases. Section 797 [5] makes it a crime to publish certain photographs or drawings of military installations. Section 798,[6] also in precise lan-

---

[4] Senator Ashurst also urged that ". . . 'freedom of the press' means freedom from the restraints of a censor, means the absolute liberty and right to publish whatever you wish; but you take your chances of punishment in the courts of your country for the violation of the laws of libel, slander and treason." 55 Cong. Rec. 2005 (1917).

[5] Section 797, 18 U. S. C., provides:

"On and after thirty days from the date upon which the President defines any vital military or naval installation or equipment as being within the category contemplated under section 795 of this title, whoever reproduces, publishes, sells, or gives away any photograph, sketch, picture, drawing, map, or graphical representation of the vital military or naval installations or equipment so defined, without first obtaining permission of the commanding officer of the military or naval post, camp, or station concerned, or higher authority, unless such photograph, sketch, picture, drawing, map, or graphical representation has clearly indicated thereon that it has been censored by the proper military or naval authority, shall be fined not more than $1,000 or imprisoned not more than one year, or both."

[6] In relevant part 18 U. S. C. § 798 provides:

"(a) Whoever knowingly and willfully communicates, furnishes, transmits, or otherwise makes available to an unauthorized person, or publishes, or uses in any manner prejudicial to the safety or inter-

guage, proscribes knowing and willful publications of any classified information concerning the cryptographic systems or communication intelligence activities of the United States as well as any information obtained from communication intelligence operations.[7] If any of the

est of the United States or for the benefit of any foreign government to the detriment of the United States any classified information—

"(1) concerning the nature, preparation, or use of any code, cipher, or cryptographic system of the United States or any foreign government; or

"(2) concerning, the design, construction, use, maintenance, or repair of any device, apparatus, or appliance used or prepared or planned for use by the United States or any foreign government for cryptographic or communication intelligence purposes; or

"(3) concerning the communication intelligence activities of the United States or any foreign government; or

"(4) obtained by the processes of communication intelligence from the communications of any foreign government, knowing the same to have been obtained by such processes—

"Shall be fined not more than $10,000 or imprisoned not more than ten years, or both."

[7] The purport of 18 U. S. C. § 798 is clear. Both the House and Senate Reports on the bill, in identical terms, speak of furthering the security of the United States by preventing disclosure of information concerning the cryptographic systems and the communication intelligence systems of the United States, and explaining that "[t]his bill makes it a crime to reveal the methods, techniques, and matériel used in the transmission by this Nation of enciphered or coded messages. . . . Further, it makes it a crime to reveal methods used by this Nation in breaking the secret codes of a foreign nation. It also prohibits under certain penalties the divulging of any information which may have come into this Government's hands as a result of such a code-breaking." H. R. Rep. No. 1895, 81st Cong., 2d Sess., 1 (1950). The narrow reach of the statute was explained as covering "only a small category of classified matter, a category which is both vital and vulnerable to an almost unique degree." *Id.,* at 2. Existing legislation was deemed inadequate.

"At present two other acts protect this information, but only in a limited way. These are the Espionage Act of 1917 (40 Stat. 217) and the act of June 10, 1933 (48 Stat. 122). Under the first, unauthorized revelation of information of this kind can be penalized only if it can be proved that the person making the revelation did

material here at issue is of this nature, the newspapers are presumably now on full notice of the position of the United States and must face the consequences if they publish. I would have no difficulty in sustaining convictions under these sections on facts that would not justify the intervention of equity and the imposition of a prior restraint.

The same would be true under those sections of the criminal code casting a wider net to protect the national defense. Section 793 (e) [8] makes it a criminal act for

---

so with an intent to injure the United States. Under the second, only diplomatic codes and messages transmitted in diplomatic codes are protected. The present bill is designed to protect against knowing and willful publication or any other revelation of all important information affecting the United States communication intelligence operations and all direct information about all United States codes and ciphers." *Ibid.*

Section 798 obviously was intended to cover publications by non-employees of the Government and to ease the Government's burden in obtaining convictions. See H. R. Rep. No. 1895, *supra,* at 2–5. The identical Senate Report, not cited in parallel in the text of this footnote, is S. Rep. No. 111, 81st Cong., 1st Sess. (1949).

[8] Section 793 (e) of 18 U. S. C. provides that:

"(e) Whoever having unauthorized possession of, access to, or control over any document, writing, code book, signal book, sketch, photograph, photographic negative, blueprint, plan, map, model, instrument, appliance, or note relating to the national defense, or information relating to the national defense which information the possessor has reason to believe could be used to the injury of the United States or to the advantage of any foreign nation, willfully communicates, delivers, transmits or causes to be communicated, delivered, or transmitted, or attempts to communicate, deliver, transmit or cause to be communicated, delivered, or transmitted the same to any person not entitled to receive it, or willfully retains the same and fails to deliver it to the officer or employee of the United States entitled to receive it;"

is guilty of an offense punishable by 10 years in prison, a $10,000 fine, or both. It should also be noted that 18 U. S. C. § 793 (g), added in 1950, see 64 Stat. 1004–1005 (1950); S. Rep. No. 2369, 81st Cong., 2d Sess., 9 (1950), provides that "[i]f two or more

any unauthorized possessor of a document "relating to national defense" either (1) willfully to communicate or cause to be communicated that document to any person not entitled to receive it or (2) willfully to retain the document and fail to deliver it to an officer of the United States entitled to receive it. The subsection was added in 1950 because pre-existing law provided no penalty for the unauthorized possessor unless demand for the documents was made.[9] "The dangers surround-

persons conspire to violate any of the foregoing provisions of this section, and one or more of such persons do any act to effect the object of the conspiracy, each of the parties to such conspiracy shall be subject to the punishment provided for the offense which is the object of such conspiracy."

[9] The amendment of § 793 that added subsection (e) was part of the Subversive Activities Control Act of 1950, which was in turn Title I of the Internal Security Act of 1950. See 64 Stat. 987 (1950). The report of the Senate Judiciary Committee best explains the purposes of the amendment:

"Section 18 of the bill amends section 793 of title 18 of the United States Code (espionage statute). The several paragraphs of section 793 of title 18 are designated as subsections (a) through (g) for purposes of convenient reference. The significant changes which would be made in section 793 of title 18 are as follows:

"(1) Amends the fourth paragraph of section 793, title 18 (subsec. (d)), to cover the unlawful dissemination of 'information relating to the national defense which information the possessor has reason to believe could be used to the injury of the United States or to the advantage of any foreign nation.' *The phrase 'which information the possessor has reason to believe could be used to the injury of the United States or to the advantage of any foreign nation' would modify only 'information relating to the national defense' and not the other items enumerated in the subsection.* The fourth paragraph of section 793 is also amended to provide that only those with lawful possession of the items relating to national defense enumerated therein may retain them subject to demand therefor. Those who have unauthorized possession of such items are treated in a separate subsection.

"(2) Amends section 793, title 18 (subsec. (e)), to provide that unauthorized possessors of items enumerated in paragraph 4 of

ing the unauthorized possession of such items are self-evident, and it is deemed advisable to require their surrender in such a case, regardless of demand, especially since their unauthorized possession may be unknown to the authorities who would otherwise make the demand." S. Rep. No. 2369, 81st Cong., 2d Sess., 9 (1950). Of

section 793 must surrender possession thereof to the proper authorities without demand. Existing law provides no penalty for the unauthorized possession of such items unless a demand for them is made by the person entitled to receive them. The dangers surrounding the unauthorized possession of such items are self-evident, and it is deemed advisable to require their surrender in such a case, regardless of demand, especially since their unauthorized possession may be unknown to the authorities who would otherwise make the demand. The only difference between subsection (d) and subsection (e) of section 793 is that a demand by the person entitled to receive the items would be a necessary element of an offense under subsection (d) where the possession is lawful, whereas such a demand would not be a necessary element of an offense under subsection (e) where the possession is unauthorized." S. Rep. No. 2369, 81st Cong., 2d Sess., 8–9 (1950) (emphasis added).

It seems clear from the foregoing, contrary to the intimations of the District Court for the Southern District of New York in this case, that in prosecuting for communicating or withholding a "document" as contrasted with similar action with respect to "information" the Government need not prove an intent to injure the United States or to benefit a foreign nation but only willful and knowing conduct. The District Court relied on *Gorin* v. *United States*, 312 U. S. 19 (1941). But that case arose under other parts of the predecessor to § 793, see 312 U. S., at 21–22—parts that imposed different intent standards not repeated in § 793 (d) or § 793 (e). Cf. 18 U. S. C. §§ 793 (a), (b), and (c). Also, from the face of subsection (e) and from the context of the act of which it was a part, it seems undeniable that a newspaper, as well as others unconnected with the Government, are vulnerable to prosecution under § 793 (e) if they communicate or withhold the materials covered by that section. The District Court ruled that "communication" did not reach publication by a newspaper of documents relating to the national defense. I intimate no views on the correctness of that conclusion. But neither communication nor publication is necessary to violate the subsection.

course, in the cases before us, the unpublished documents have been demanded by the United States and their import has been made known at least to counsel for the newspapers involved. In *Gorin* v. *United States,* 312 U. S. 19, 28 (1941), the words "national defense" as used in a predecessor of § 793 were held by a unanimous court to have "a well understood connotation"— a "generic concept of broad connotations, referring to the military and naval establishments and the related activities of national preparedness"—and to be "sufficiently definite to apprise the public of prohibited activities" and to be consonant with due process. 312 U. S., at 28. Also, as construed by the Court in *Gorin,* information "connected with the national defense" is obviously not limited to that threatening "grave and irreparable" injury to the United States.[10]

It is thus clear that Congress has addressed itself to the problems of protecting the security of the country and the national defense from unauthorized disclosure of potentially damaging information. Cf. *Youngstown Sheet & Tube Co.* v. *Sawyer,* 343 U. S. 579, 585–586 (1952); see also *id.,* at 593–628 (Frankfurter, J., concurring). It has not, however, authorized the injunctive remedy against threatened publication. It has apparently been satisfied to rely on criminal sanctions and their deterrent effect on the responsible as well as the irresponsible press. I am not, of course, saying that either of these newspapers has yet committed a crime

---

[10] Also relevant is 18 U. S. C. § 794. Subsection (b) thereof forbids in time of war the collection or publication, with intent that it shall be communicated to the enemy, any information with respect to the movements of military forces, "or with respect to the plans or conduct . . . of any naval or military operations . . . or any other information relating to the public defense, which might be useful to the enemy . . . ."

or that either would commit a crime if they published all the material now in their possession. That matter must await resolution in the context of a criminal proceeding if one is instituted by the United States. In that event, the issue of guilt or innocence would be determined by procedures and standards quite different from those that have purported to govern these injunctive proceedings.

SUPREME COURT OF THE UNITED STATES

Nos. 1873 AND 1885.—OCTOBER TERM, 1970

New York Times Company, Petitioner, 1873 v. United States.	On Writ of Certiorari to the United States Court of Appeals for the Second Circuit.
United States, Petitioner, 1885 v. The Washington Post Company et al.	On Writ of Certiorari to the United States Court of Appeals for the District of Columbia Circuit.

[June 30, 1971]

MR. JUSTICE MARSHALL, concurring.

The Government contends that the only issue in this case is whether in a suit by the United States, "the First Amendment bars a court from prohibiting a newspaper from publishing material whose disclosure would pose a grave and immediate danger to the security of the United States." Brief of the Government, at 6. With all due respect, I believe the ultimate issue in this case is even more basic than the one posed by the Solicitor General. The issue is whether this Court or the Congress has the power to make law.

In this case there is no problem concerning the President's power to classify information as "secret" or "top secret." Congress has specifically recognized Presidential authority, which has been formally exercised in Executive Order 10501, to classify documents and information. See, e. g., 18 U. S. C. § 798; 50 U. S. C. § 783.[1] Nor is there any issue here regarding the President's power as Chief Executive and Commander-in-Chief to

---

[1] See n. 3, *infra.*

protect national security by disciplining employees who disclose information and by taking precautions to prevent leaks.

The problem here is whether in this particular case the Executive Branch has authority to invoke the equity jurisdiction of the courts to protect what it believes to be the national interest. See *In re Debs,* 158 U. S. 564, 584 (1895). The Government argues that in addition to the inherent power of any government to protect itself, the President's power to conduct foreign affairs and his position as Commander-in-Chief give him authority to impose censorship on the press to protect his ability to deal effectively with foreign nations and to conduct the military affairs of the country. Of course, it is beyond cavil that the President has broad powers by virtue of his primary responsibility for the conduct of our foreign affairs and his position as Commander-in-Chief. *Chicago & Southern Air Lines, Inc.* v. *Waterman Corp.,* 333 U. S. 103 (1948); *Hirabayashi* v. *United States,* 320 U. S. 81, 93 (1943); *United States* v. *Curtiss-Wright Export Co.,* 299 U. S. 304 (1936).[2] And in some situations it may be that under whatever inherent powers the Government may have, as well as the implicit authority derived from the President's mandate to conduct foreign affairs and to act as Commander-in-Chief there is a basis for the invocation of the equity jurisdiction of this Court as an aid to prevent the publication of material damaging to "national security," however that term may be defined.

It would, however, be utterly inconsistent with the concept of separation of power for this Court to use its power of contempt to prevent behavior that Congress has

---

[2] But see *Kent* v. *Dulles,* 357 U. S. 116 (1958); *Youngstown Sheet & Tube Co.* v. *Sawyer,* 343 U. S. 579 (1952).

specifically declined to prohibit. There would be a similar damage to the basic concept of these coequal branches of Government if when the Executive has adequate authority granted by Congress to protect "national security" it can choose instead to invoke the contempt power of a court to enjoin the threatened conduct. The Constitution provides that Congress shall make laws, the President execute laws, and courts interpret law. *Youngstown Sheet & Tube Co.* v. *Sawyer,* 343 U. S. 579 (1952). It did not provide for government by injunction in which the courts and the Executive can "make law" without regard to the action of Congress. It may be more convenient for the Executive if it need only convince a judge to prohibit conduct rather than to ask the Congress to pass a law and it may be more convenient to enforce a contempt order than seek a criminal conviction in a jury trial. Moreover, it may be considered politically wise to get a court to share the responsibility for arresting those who the Executive has probable cause to believe are violating the law. But convenience and political considerations of the moment do not justify a basic departure from the principles of our system of government.

In this case we are not faced with a situation where Congress has failed to provide the Executive with broad power to protect the Nation from disclosure of damaging state secrets. Congress has on several occasions given extensive consideration to the problem of protecting the military and strategic secrets of the United States. This consideration has resulted in the enactment of statutes making it a crime to receive, disclose, communicate, withhold, and publish certain documents, photographs, instruments, appliances, and information. The bulk of these statutes are found to chapter 37 of U. S. C., Title 18, entitled Espionage and Censorship.[3]   In that chapter, Congress has provided penalties ranging from a $10,000 fine to death for violating the various statutes.

Thus it would seem that in order for this Court to issue an injunction it would require a showing that such

---

[3] There are several other statutory provisions prohibiting and punishing the dissemination of information, the disclosure of which Congress thought sufficiently imperiled national security to warrant that result.   These include 42 U. S. C. §§ 2161 through 2166 relating to the authority of the Atomic Energy Commission to classify and declassify "Restricted Data" ["Restricted Data" is a term of art employed uniquely by the Atomic Energy Act].   Specifically, 42 U. S. C. § 2162 authorizes the Atomic Energy Commission to classify certain information.   42 U. S. C. § 2274, subsection (a) provides penalties for a person who "communicates, transmits, or discloses . . . with intent to injure the United States or an intent to secure an advantage to any foreign nation. . . ."   "Restricted Data."   Subsection (b) of § 2274 provides lesser penalties for one who "communicates, transmits, or discloses" such information "with reason to believe such data will be utilized to injure the United States or to secure an advantage to any foreign nation . . . ."   Other sections of Title 42 of the U. S. C. dealing with atomic energy prohibit and punish acquisition, removal, concealment, tampering with, alteration, mutilation, or destruction of documents incorporating "Restricted Data" and provide penalties for employees and former employees of the Atomic Energy Commission, the armed services, contractors and licensees of the Atomic Energy Commission.   42 U. S. C. §§ 2276, 2277.   Title 50 U. S. C. Appendix § 781 (part of the National Defense Act of 1941, as amended, 55 Stat. 236) prohibits the making of any sketch or other representation of military installations or any military equipment located on any military installation, as specified; and indeed Congress in the National Defense Act conferred jurisdiction on federal district courts over civil actions "to enjoin any violation" thereof.   50 U. S. C. App. § 1152.   50 U. S. C. § 783 (b) makes it unlawful for any officers or employees of the United States or any corporation which is owned by the United States to communicate material which has been "classified" by the President to any person whom that governmental employee knows or has reason to believe is an agent or representative of any foreign government or any Communist organization.

an injunction would enhance the already existing power of the Government to act. See *Bennett* v. *Laman,* 277 N. Y. 368, 14 N. E. 2d 439 (1938). It is a traditional axiom of equity that a court of equity will not do a useless thing just as it is a traditional axiom that equity will not enjoin the commission of a crime. See Z. Chaffe & E. Re, Equity 935–954 (5th ed. 1967); 1 H. Joyce, Injunctions §§ 58–60a (1909). Here there has been no attempt to make such a showing. The Solicitor General does not even mention in his brief whether the Government considers there to be probable cause to believe a crime has been committed or whether there is a conspiracy to commit future crimes.

If the Government had attempted to show that there was no effective remedy under traditional criminal law, it would have had to show that there is no arguably applicable statute. Of course, at this stage this Court could not and cannot determine whether there has been a violation of a particular statute nor decide the constitutionality of any statute. Whether a good-faith prosecution could have been instituted under any statute could, however, be determined.

At least one of the many statutes in this area seems relevant to this case. Congress has provided in 18 U. S. C. § 793 (e) that whoever "having unauthorized possession of, access to, or control over any document, writing, code book, signal book . . . or note relating to the national defense, or information relating to the national defense which information the possessor has reason to believe could be used to the injury of the United States or to the advantage of any foreign nation, willfully communicates, delivers, transmits . . . the same to any person not entitled to receive it, or willfully retains the same and fails to deliver it to the officer or employee of the United States entitled to receive it . . . shall be fined not more than $10,000 or imprisoned not more than ten years, or both."

18 U. S. C. § 793 (e).   Congress has also made it a crime to conspire to commit any of the offenses listed in 18 U. S. C. § 793 (e).

It is true that Judge Gurfein found that Congress had not made it a crime to publish the items and material specified in § 793 (e): He found that the words "communicates, delivers, transmits . . ." did not refer to publication of newspaper stories.   And that view has some support in the legislative history and conforms with the past practice of using the statute only to prosecute those charged with ordinary espionage.   But see 103 Cong. Rec. 10449 (remarks of Sen. Humphrey).   Judge Gurfein's view of the statute is not, however, the only plausible construction that could be given.   See my Brother WHITE's concurring opinion.

Even if it is determined that the Government could not in good faith bring criminal prosecutions against the New York Times and the Washington Post, it is clear that Congress has specifically rejected passing legislation that would have clearly given the President the power he seeks here and made the current activity of the newspapers unlawful.   When Congress specifically declines to make conduct unlawful it is not for this Court to redecide those issues—to overrule Congress.   See *Youngstown Sheet & Tube* v. *Sawyer*, 345 U. S. 579 (1952).

On at least two occasions Congress has refused to enact legislation that would have made the conduct engaged in here unlawful and given the President the power that he seeks in this case.   In 1917 during the debate over the original Espionage Act, still the basic provisions of § 793, Congress rejected a proposal to give the President in time of war or threat of war authority to directly prohibit by proclamation the publication of information relating to national defense that might be useful to the enemy. The proposal provided that:

"During any national emergency resulting from a war to which the United States is a party, or from threat of such a war, the President may, by proclamation, prohibit the publishing or communicating of, or the attempting to publish or communicate any information relating to the national defense which, in his judgment, is of such character that it is or might be useful to the enemy. Whoever violates any such prohibition shall be punished by a fine of not more than $10,000 or by imprisonment for not more than 10 years, or both: *Provided,* That nothing in this section shall be construed to limit or restrict any discussion, comment, or criticism of the acts or policies of the Government or its representatives or the publication of the same." 55 Cong. Rec. 1763.

Congress rejected this proposal after war against Germany had been declared even though many believed that there was a grave national emergency and that the threat of security leaks and espionage were serious. The Executive has not gone to Congress and requested that the decision to provide such power be reconsidered. Instead, the Executive comes to this Court and asks that it be granted the power Congress refused to give.

In 1957 the United States Commission on Government Security found that "[a]irplane journals, scientific periodicals, and even the daily newspaper have featured articles containing information and other data which should have ben deleted in whole or in part for security reasons." In response to this problem the Commission, which was chaired by Senator Cotton, proposed that "Congress enact legislation making it a crime for any person willfully to disclose without proper authorization, for any purpose whatever, information classified 'secret' or 'top secret,' knowing, or having reasonable grounds to believe, such information to have been so classified." Report of Commission on Government Security 619–620 (1957). After substantial floor discussion on the proposal, it was rejected. See 103 Cong. Rec. 10447–10450. If the proposal that Senator Cotton championed on the floor had been enacted, the publication of the documents involved here would certainly have been a crime. Congress refused, however, to make it a crime. The Government is here asking this Court to remake that decision. This Court has no such power.

Either the Government has the power under statutory grant to use traditional criminal law to protect the country or, if there is no basis for arguing that Congress has made the activity a crime, it is plain that Congress has specifically refused to grant the authority the Government seeks from this Court. In either case this Court does not have authority to grant the requested relief. It is not for this Court to fling itself into every breach perceived by some Government official nor is it for this Court to take on itself the burden of enacting law, especially law that Congress has refused to pass.

I believe that the judgment of the United States Court of Appeals for the District of Columbia should be affirmed and the judgment of the United States Court of Appeals for the Second Circuit should be reversed insofar as it remands the case for further hearings.

SUPREME COURT OF THE UNITED STATES

Nos. 1873 AND 1885.—OCTOBER TERM, 1970

New York Times Company, Petitioner, 1873 _v._ United States. } On Writ of Certiorari to the United States Court of Appeals for the Second Circuit.

United States, Petitioner, 1885 _v._ The Washington Post Company et al. } On Writ of Certiorari to the United States Court of Appeals for the District of Columbia Circuit.

[June 30, 1971]

MR. CHIEF JUSTICE BURGER, dissenting.

So clear are the constitutional limitations on prior restraint against expression, that from the time of _Near_ v. _Minnesota_, 283 U. S. 697 (1931), until recently in _Organization for a Better Austin_ v. _Keefe_, —— U. S. —— (1971), we have had little occasion to be concerned with cases involving prior restraints against news reporting on matters of public interest. There is, therefore, little variation among the members of the Court in terms of resistance to prior restraints against publication. Adherence to this basic constitutional principle, however, does not make this case a simple one. In this case, the imperative of a free and unfettered press comes into collision with another imperative, the effective functioning of a complex modern government and specifically the effective exercise of certain constitutional powers of the Executive. Only those who view the First Amendment as an absolute in all circumstances—a view I respect, but reject—can find such a case as this to be simple or easy.

This case is not simple for another and more immediate reason. We do not know the facts of the case. No District Judge knew all the facts. No Court of Appeals judge knew all the facts. No member of this Court knows all the facts.

Why are we in this posture, in which only those judges to whom the First Amendment is absolute and permits of no restraint in any circumstances or for any reason, are really in a position to act?

I suggest we are in this posture because these cases have been conducted in unseemly haste. MR. JUSTICE HARLAN covers the chronology of events demonstrating the hectic pressures under which these cases have been processed and I need not restate them. The prompt setting of these cases reflects our universal abhorrence of prior restraint. But prompt judicial action does not mean unjudicial haste.

Here, moreover, the frenetic haste is due in large part to the manner in which the *Times* proceeded from the date it obtained the purloined documents. It seems reasonably clear now that the haste precluded reasonable and deliberate judicial treatment of these cases and was not warranted. The precipitous action of this Court aborting a trial not yet completed is not the kind of judicial conduct which ought to attend the disposition of a great issue.

The newspapers make a derivative claim under the First Amendment; they denominate this right as the public right-to-know; by implication, the *Times* asserts a sole trusteeship of that right by virtue of its journalist "scoop." The right is asserted as an absolute. Of course, the First Amendment right itself is not an absolute, as Justice Holmes so long ago pointed out in his aphorism concerning the right to shout of fire in a crowded theater. There are other exceptions, some of which Chief Justice Hughes mentioned by way of example in *Near* v. *Minnesota*. There are no doubt other exceptions no one has had occasion to describe or discuss. Conceivably such exceptions may be lurking in these cases and would have been flushed had they been properly considered in the trial courts, free from unwarranted deadlines and frenetic pressures. A great issue of this kind should be tried in a judicial atmosphere conducive to thoughtful, reflective deliberation, especially when haste, in terms of hours, is unwarranted in light of the long period the *Times,* by its own choice, deferred publication.

It is not disputed that the *Times* has had unauthorized possession of the documents for three to four months, during which it has had its expert analysts studying them, presumably digesting them and preparing the material for publication. During all of this time, the *Times,* presumably in its capacity as trustee of the public's "right to know," has held up publication for purposes it considered proper and thus public knowledge was delayed. No doubt this was for a good reason; the analysis of 7,000 pages of complex material drawn from a vastly greater volume of material would inevitably take time and the writing of good news stories takes time. But why should the United States Government, from whom this information was illegally acquired by someone, along with all the counsel, trial judges, and appellate judges be placed under needless pressure? After these months of deferral, the alleged right-to-know has somehow and suddenly become a right that must be vindicated instanter.

Would it have been unreasonable, since the newspaper could anticipate the government's objections to release of secret material, to give the government an opportunity to review the entire collection and determine whether agreement could be reached on publication? Stolen or not, if security was not in fact jeopardized, much of the material could no doubt have been declassified, since it spans a period ending in 1968. With such an approach— one that great newspapers have in the past practiced and

stated editorially to be the duty of an honorable press—
the newspapers and government might well have nar-
rowed the area of disagreement as to what was and was
not publishable, leaving the remainder to be resolved in
orderly litigation if necessary.   To me it is hardly be-
lievable that a newspaper long regarded as a great institution in American life would fail to perform one of
the basic and simple duties of every citizen with respect
to the discovery or possession of stolen property or secret
government documents.   That duty, I had thought—perhaps naively—was to report forthwith, to responsible
public officers.   This duty rests on taxi drivers, Justices
and the New York Times.   The course followed by the
Times, whether so calculated or not, removed any possibility of orderly litigation of the issues.   If the action
of the judges up to now has been correct, that result is
sheer happenstance.[1]

Our grant of the writ before final judgment in the *Times*
case aborted the trial in the District Court before it had
made a complete record pursuant to the mandate of the
Court of Appeals, Second Circuit.

The consequence of all this melancholy series of events
is that we literally do not know what we are acting on.
As I see it we have been forced to deal with litigation
concerning rights of great magnitude without an adequate record, and surely without time for adequate treatment either in the prior proceedings or in this Court.
It is interesting to note that counsel in oral argument
before this Court were frequently unable to respond to
questions on factual points.   Not surprisingly they
pointed out that they had been working literally "around

---

[1] Interestingly the *Times* explained its refusal to allow the government to examine its own purloined documents by saying in substance
this might compromise *their* sources and informants!   The *Times*
thus asserts a right to guard the secrecy of its sources while denying
that the Government of the United States has that power.

the clock" and simply were unable to review the documents that give rise to these cases and were not familiar with them.   This Court is in no better posture.   I agree with MR. JUSTICE HARLAN and MR. JUSTICE BLACKMUN but I am not prepared to reach the merits.[2]

I would affirm the Court of Appeals for the Second Circuit and allow the District Court to complete the trial aborted by our grant of certiorari meanwhile preserving the *status quo* in the *Post* case.   I would direct that the District Court on remand give priority to the *Times* case to the exclusion of all other business of that court but I would not set arbitrary deadlines.

I should add that I am in general agreement with much of what MR. JUSTICE WHITE has expressed with respect to penal sanctions concerning communication or retention of documents or information relating to the national defense.

We all crave speedier judicial processes but when judges are pressured as in these cases the result is a parody of the judicial process.

---

[2] With respect to the question of inherent power of the Executive to classify papers, records and documents as secret, or otherwise unavailable for public exposure, and to secure aid of the courts for enforcement, there may be an analogy with respect to this Court. No statute gives this Court express power to establish and enforce the utmost security measures for the secrecy of our deliberations and records.   Yet I have little doubt as to the inherent power of the Court to protect the confidentiality of its internal operations by whatever judicial measures may be required.

SUPREME COURT OF THE UNITED STATES

Nos. 1873 AND 1885.—OCTOBER TERM, 1970

New York Times Company, Petitioner, 1873 v. United States.	On Writ of Certiorari to the United States Court of Appeals for the Second Circuit.

United States, Petitioner, 1885 v. The Washington Post Company et al.	On Writ of Certiorari to the United States Court of Appeals for the District of Columbia Circuit.

[June 30, 1971]

MR. JUSTICE HARLAN, with whom THE CHIEF JUSTICE and MR. JUSTICE BLACKMUN join, dissenting.

These cases forcefully call to mind the wise admonition of Mr. Justice Holmes, dissenting in *Northern Securities Co.* v. *United States*, 193 U. S. 197, 400–401 (1904):

> "Great cases like hard cases make bad law. For great cases are called great, not by reason of their real importance in shaping the law of the future, but because of some accident of immediate overwhelming interest which appeals to the feelings and distorts the judgment. These immediate interests exercise a kind of hydraulic pressure which makes what previously was clear seem doubtful, and before which even well settled principles of law will bend."

With all respect, I consider that the Court has been almost irresponsibly feverish in dealing with these cases.

Both the Court of Appeals for the Second Circuit and the Court of Appeals for the District of Columbia Circuit rendered judgment on June 23. The New York Times' petition for certiorari, its motion for accelerated consideration thereof, and its application for interim relief were filed in this Court on June 24 at about 11 a. m.   The application of the United States for interim relief in the *Post* case was also filed here on June 24, at about 7:15 p. m.   This Court's order setting a hearing before us on June 26 at 11 a. m., a course which I joined only to avoid the possibility of even more peremptory action by the Court, was issued less than 24 hours before.   The record in the *Post* case was filed with the Clerk shortly before 1 p. m. on June 25; the record in the *Times* case did not arrive until 7 or 8 o'clock that same night.   The briefs of the parties were received less than two hours before argument on June 26.

This frenzied train of events took place in the name of the presumption against prior restraints created by the First Amendment.   Due regard for the extraordinarily important and difficult questions involved in these litigations should have led the Court to shun such a precipitate timetable.   In order to decide the merits of these cases properly, some or all of the following questions should have been faced:

1. Whether the Attorney General is authorized to bring these suits in the name of the United States.   Compare *In re Debs,* 158 U. S. 564 (1895), with *Youngstown Sheet & Tube Co.* v. *Sawyer,* 343 U. S. 579 (1952).   This question involves as well the construction and validity of a singularly opaque statute—the Espionage Act, 18 U. S. C. § 793 (e).

2. Whether the First Amendment permits the federal courts to enjoin publication of stories which would present a serious threat to national security.   See *Near* v. *Minnesota,* 283 U. S. 697, 716 (1931) (dictum).

3. Whether the threat to publish highly secret documents is of itself a sufficient implication of national security to justify an injunction on the theory that regardless of the contents of the documents harm enough results

simply from the demonstration of such a breach of secrecy.

4. Whether the unauthorized disclosure of any of these particular documents would seriously impair the national security.

5. What weight should be given to the opinion of high officers in the Executive Branch of the Government with respect to questions 3 and 4.

6. Whether the newspapers are entitled to retain and use the documents notwithstanding the seemingly uncontested facts that the documents, or the originals of which they are duplicates, were purloined from the Government's possession and that the newspapers received them with knowledge that they had been feloniously acquired. Cf. *Liberty Lobby, Inc.* v. *Pearson,* 390 F. 2d 489 (CADC 1968).

7. Whether the threatened harm to the national security or the Government's possessory interest in the documents justifies the issuance of an injunction against publication in light of—

a. The strong First Amendment policy against prior restraints on publication;

b. The doctrine against enjoining conduct in violation of criminal statutes; and

c. The extent to which the materials at issue have apparently already been otherwise disseminated.

These are difficult questions of fact, of law, and of judgment; the potential consequences of erroneous decision are enormous. The time which has been available to us, to the lower courts,* and to the parties has been

---

*The hearing in the *Post* case before Judge Gesell began at 8 a. m. on June 21, and his decision was rendered, under the hammer of a deadline imposed by the Court of Appeals, shortly before 5 p. m. on the same day. The hearing in the *Times* case before Judge Gurfein was held on June 18 and his decision was rendered on June 19. The Government's appeals in the two cases were heard by the Courts

wholly inadequate for giving these cases the kind of consideration they deserve. It is a reflection on the stability of the judicial process that these great issues—as important as any that have arisen during my time on the Court—should have been decided under the pressures engendered by the torrent of publicity that has attended' these litigations from their inception.

Forced as I am to reach the merits of these cases, I dissent from the opinion and judgments of the Court. Within the severe limitations imposed by the time constraints under which I have been required to operate, I can only state my reasons in telescoped form, even though in different circumstances I would have felt constrained to deal with the cases in the fuller sweep indicated above.

It is a sufficient basis for affirming the Court of Appeals for the Second Circuit in the *Times* litigation to observe that its order must rest on the conclusion that because of the time elements the Government had not been given an adequate opportunity to present its case to the District Court. At the least this conclusion was not an abuse of discretion.

In the *Post* litigation the Government had more time to prepare; this was apparently the basis for the refusal of the Court of Appeals for the District of Columbia Circuit on rehearing to conform its judgment to that of the Second Circuit. But I think there is another and more fundamental reason why this judgment cannot stand—a reason which also furnishes an additional ground for not reinstating the judgment of the District Court in the *Times* litigation, set aside by the Court of Appeals. It is plain to me that the scope of the judicial function in passing upon the activities of the Executive

----

of Appeals for the District of Columbia and Second Circuits, each court sitting *en banc*, on June 22. Each court rendered its decision on the following afternoon.

Branch of the Government in the field of foreign affairs is very narrowly restricted. This view is, I think, dictated by the concept of separation of powers upon which our constitutional system rests.

In a speech on the floor of the House of Representatives, Chief Justice John Marshall, then a member of that body, stated:

> "The President is the sole organ of the nation in its external relations, and its sole representative with foreign nations." Annals, 6th Cong., col. 613 (1800).

From that time, shortly after the founding of the Nation, to this, there has been no substantial challenge to this description of the scope of executive power. See *United States* v. *Curtiss-Wright Export Corp.*, 299 U. S. 304, 319–321 (1936), collecting authorities.

From this constitutional primacy in the field of foreign affairs, it seems to me that certain conclusions necessarily follow. Some of these were stated concisely by President Washington, declining the request of the House of Representatives for the papers leading up to the negotiation of the Jay Treaty:

> "The nature of foreign negotiations requires caution, and their success must often depend on secrecy; and even when brought to a conclusion a full disclosure of all the measures, demands, or eventual concessions which may have been proposed or contemplated would be extremely impolitic; for this might have a pernicious influence on future negotiations, or produce immediate inconveniences, perhaps danger and mischief, in relation to other powers." 1 J. Richardson, Messages and Papers of the Presidents 194–195 (1899).

The power to evaluate the "pernicious influence" of premature disclosure is not, however, lodged in the Executive alone. I agree that, in performance of its duty to protect the values of the First Amendment against political pressures, the judiciary must review the initial Executive determination to the point of satisfying itself that the subject matter of the dispute does lie within the proper compass of the President's foreign relations power. Constitutional considerations forbid "a complete abandonment of judicial control." Cf. *United States* v. *Reynolds*, 345 U. S. 1, 8 (1953). Moreover, the judiciary may properly insist that the determination that disclosure of the subject matter would irreparably impair the national security be made by the head of the Executive Department concerned—here the Secretary of State or the Secretary of Defense—after actual personal consideration by that officer. This safeguard is required in the analogous area of executive claims of privilege for secrets of state. See *United States* v. *Reynolds*, *supra*, at 8 and n. 20; *Duncan* v. *Cammell, Laird & Co.*, [1942] A. C. 624, 638 (House of Lords).

But in my judgment the judiciary may not properly go beyond these two inquiries and redetermine for itself the probable impact of disclosure on the national security.

> "[T]he very nature of executive decisions as to foreign policy is political, not judicial. Such decisions are wholly confided by our Constitution to the political departments of the government, Executive and Legislative. They are delicate, complex, and involve large elements of prophecy. They are and should be undertaken only by those directly responsible to the people whose welfare they advance or imperil. They are decisions of a kind for which the Judiciary has neither aptitude, facilities nor responsibility and which has long been held to belong in the domain of political power not subject to judicial intrusion or inquiry." *Chicago & Southern*

Air Lines v. *Waterman Steamship Corp.*, 333 U. S. 103, 111 (1948) (Jackson, J.).

Even if there is some room for the judiciary to override the executive determination, it is plain that the scope of review must be exceedingly narrow. I can see no indication in the opinions of either the District Court or the Court of Appeals in the *Post* litigation that the conclusions of the Executive were given even the deference owing to an administrative agency, much less that owing to a co-equal branch of the Government operating within the field of its constitutional prerogative.

Accordingly, I would vacate the judgment of the Court of Appeals for the District of Columbia Circuit on this ground and remand the case for further proceedings in the District Court. Before the commencement of such further proceedings, due opportunity should be afforded the Government for procuring from the Secretary of State or the Secretary of Defense or both an expression of their views on the issue of national security. The ensuing review by the District Court should be in accordance with the views expressed in this opinion. And for the reasons stated above I would affirm the judgment of the Court of Appeals for the Second Circuit.

Pending further hearings in each case conducted under the appropriate ground rules, I would continue the restraints on publication. I cannot believe that the doctrine prohibiting prior restraints reaches to the point of preventing courts from maintaining the *status quo* long enough to act responsibly in matters of such national importance as those involved here.

SUPREME COURT OF THE UNITED STATES

Nos. 1873 AND 1885.—OCTOBER TERM, 1970

New York Times Company, Petitioner, 1873 *v.* United States. } On Writ of Certiorari to the United States Court of Appeals for the Second Circuit.

United States, Petitioner, 1885 *v.* The Washington Post Company et al. } On Writ of Certiorari to the United States Court of Appeals for the District of Columbia Circuit.

[June 30, 1971]

MR. JUSTICE BLACKMUN.

I join MR. JUSTICE HARLAN in his dissent. I also am in substantial accord with much that MR. JUSTICE WHITE says, by way of admonition, in the latter part of his opinion.

At this point the focus is on *only* the comparatively few documents specified by the Government as critical. So far as the other material—vast in amount—is concerned, let it be published and published forthwith if the newspapers, once the strain is gone and the sensationalism is eased, still feel the urge so to do.

But we are concerned here with the few documents specified from the 47 volumes. Almost 70 years ago Mr. Justice Holmes, dissenting in a celebrated case, observed:

> "Great cases like hard cases make bad law. For great cases are called great, not by reason of their real importance in shaping the law of the future, but because of some accident of immediate overwhelming interest which appeals to the feelings and distorts the judgment. These immediate interests exercise a kind of hydraulic pressure . . . ." *Northern Securities Co.* v. *United States,* 193 U. S. 197, 400–401 (1904).

The present cases, if not great, are at least unusual in their posture and implications, and the Holmes observation certainly has pertinent application.

The New York Times clandestinely devoted a period of three months examining the 47 volumes that came into its unauthorized possession. Once it had begun publication of material from those volumes, the New York case now before us emerged. It immediately assumed, and ever since has maintained, a frenetic pace and character. Seemingly, once publication started, the material could not be made public fast enough. Seemingly, from then on, every deferral or delay, by restraint or otherwise, was abhorrent and was to be deemed violative of the First Amendment and of the public's "right immediately to know." Yet that newspaper stood before us at oral argument and professed criticism of the Government for not lodging its protest earlier than by a Monday telegram following the initial Sunday publication.

The District of Columbia case is much the same.

Two federal district courts, two United States courts of appeals, and this Court—within a period of less than three weeks from inception until today—have been pressed into hurried decision of profound constitutional issues on inadequately developed and largely assumed facts without the careful deliberation that, hopefully, should characterize the American judicial process. There has been much writing about the law and little knowledge and less digestion of the facts. In the New York case the judges, both trial and appellate, had not yet examined the basic material when the case was brought here. In the District of Columbia case, little more was done, and what was accomplished in this respect was only on required remand, with the Washington Post, on the excuse that it was trying to protect its source of information, initially refusing to reveal what material it actually possessed, and with the district court forced to make assumptions as to that possession.

With such respect as may be due to the contrary view, this, in my opinon, is not the way to try a law suit of this magnitude and asserted importance. It is not the way for federal courts to adjudicate, and to be required to adjudicate, issues that allegedly concern the Nation's vital welfare. The country would be none the worse off were the cases tried quickly, to be sure, but in the customary and properly deliberative manner. The most recent of the material, it is said, dates no later than 1968, already about three years ago, and the Times itself took three months to formulate its plan of procedure and, thus, deprived its public for that period.

The First Amendment, after all, is only one part of an entire Constitution. Article II of the great document vests in the Executive Branch primary power over the conduct of foreign affairs and places in that branch the responsibility for the Nation's safety. Each provision of the Constitution is important, and I cannot subscribe to a doctrine of unlimited absolutism for the First Amendment at the cost of downgrading other provisions. First Amendment absolutism has never commanded a majority of this Court. See, for example, *Near* v. *Minnesota,* 283 U. S. 697, 708 (1931), and *Schenck* v. *United States,* 249 U. S. 47, 52 (1919). What is needed here is a weighing, upon properly developed standards, of the broad right of the press to print and of the very narrow right of the Government to prevent. Such standards are not yet developed. The parties here are in disagreement as to what those standards should be. But even the newspapers concede that there are situations where restraint is in order and is constitutional. Mr. Justice Holmes gave us a suggestion when he said in *Schenck,*

> "It is a question of proximity and degree. When a nation is at war many things that might be said in time of peace are such a hindrance to its effort that their utterance will not be endured so long as men

fight and that no Court could regard them as protected by any constitutional right." 249 U. S., at 52.

I therefore would remand these cases to be developed expeditiously, of course, but on a schedule permitting the orderly presentation of evidence from both sides, with the use of discovery, if necessary, as authorized by the rules, and with the preparation of briefs, oral argument and court opinions of a quality better than has been seen to this point. In making this last statement, I criticize no lawyer or judge. I know from past personal experience the agony of time pressure in the preparation of litigation. But these cases and the issues involved and the courts, including this one, deserve better than has been produced thus far.

It may well be that if these cases were allowed to develop as they should be developed, and to be tried as lawyers should try them and as courts should hear them, free of pressure and panic and sensationalism, other light would be shed on the situation and contrary considerations, for me, might prevail. But that is not the present posture of the litigation.

The Court, however, decides the cases today the other way. I therefore add one final comment.

I strongly urge, and sincerely hope, that these two newspapers will be fully aware of their ultimate responsibilities to the United States of America. Judge Wilkey, dissenting in the District of Columbia case, after a review of only the affidavits before his court (the basic papers had not then been made available by either party), concluded that there were a number of examples of documents that, if in the possession of the Post, and if published, "could clearly result in great harm to the nation," and he defined "harm" to mean "the death of soldiers, the destruction of alliances, the greatly increased difficulty of negotiation with our enemies, the inability of our diplomats to negotiate . . . ." I, for one, have now been able to give at least some cursory study not only to the affidavits, but to the material itself. I regret to say that from this examination I fear that Judge Wilkey's statements have possible foundation. I therefore share his concern. I hope that damage already has not been done. If, however, damage has been done, and if, with the Court's action today, these newspapers proceed to publish the critical documents and there results therefrom "the death of soldiers, the destruction of alliances, the greatly increased difficulty of negotiation with our enemies, the inability of our diplomats to negotiate," to which list I might add the factors of prolongation of the war and of further delay in the freeing of United States prisoners, then the Nation's people will know where the responsibility for these sad consequences rests.

134   NEW YORK TIMES CO. *v.* UNITED STATES

The judgment of the Court of Appeals for the District of Columbia Circuit is therefore affirmed. The order of the Court of Appeals for the Second Circuit is reversed and the case is remanded with directions to enter a judgment affirming the judgment of the District Court for the Southern District of New York. The stays entered June 25, 1971, by the Court are vacated. The judgments shall issue forthwith.

So ordered.